MASS VIOLENCE IN AMERICA

ILLEGAL PRACTICES

OF THE DEPARTMENT OF JUSTICE

R. G. Brown, Zechariah Chafee, Jr., et al.

ARNO PRESS & THE NEW YORK TIMES

New York • 1969

Editorial Note

Nations, like men, are sometimes interested in burying the past.

In early 1968, after more than five years marked by political assassinations, racial uprisings, campus disorders, mass demonstrations and the violent suppression of protest, *The New York Times Magazine* asked a group of distinguished scholars to reply to the question, "Is America by nature a violent society?" In answer, University of Chicago anthropologist Clifford Geertz wrote:

"We do not know very well what kind of society we live in, what kind of history we have had, what kind of people we are. We are just now beginning to find out, the hard way . . ."

The proposition was astonishing but correct: what was least understood about domestic political violence was its role in American history. It was common knowledge that the United States had had a Revolution, a Civil War, some trouble with the Indians and a period of labor-management conflict. But one could search the shelves of the nation's great libraries without discovering more than a handful of works on the subject of violence in American history, and these hopelessly out of date.

Historians had generally ignored or soft-pedaled the history of farmer uprisings, native vigilantism, labor-management struggles, ethnic conflicts and race riots; comparative work in the history of social conflict was particularly weak. Sociologists and political scientists in the grip of "consensus" theory tended to treat episodes of mass violence in America as insignificant or aberrational—temporary exceptions to the norm of peaceful progress. Psychologists and behavioral scientists discussed "mob violence" in terms which suggested that riots, revolts, insurrections and official violence were the products of individual or group pathology. All such interpretations had the effect not only of minimizing group violence in America, but of depriving it of political content—hence, of relevance to the present.

As a result, as late as 1968, the rich, multifarious and often terrifying history of domestic political violence was still largely *terra incognita*. So long as most Americans wished to keep certain skeletons locked away in their closets, few scholars would attempt to open doors. Conversely, once the American people, frightened yet emboldened by the sudden reappearance of intense social conflict, began to ask new questions about the past, so did the scholars.

Our purpose in helping Arno Press and *The New York Times* select and publish significant documents in the history of political violence has not been to compound past errors by overemphasizing the role of conflict in American history. On the contrary, our aim has been to provide materials which will aid in the search for an accurate perspective on the present. MASS VIOLENCE IN AMERICA includes eyewitness reports, government documents and other descriptive and analytic material relating to mass political violence in the United States. These documents not only provide information—they give the "feel" or "flavor" of past eras of civil disorder by evoking the emotional and political context in which revolts took place. Most of them have long been out of print and are obtainable, if at all, only in the nation's largest libraries.

The scope of this series is wide, ranging from accounts of Indian warfare to descriptions of labor-management violence, from narratives of colonial insurrections to reports on modern racial uprisings. It is not, however, limitless, nor were the constituent volumes carelessly selected. The principle of coherence which guided the selections is implicit in the phrase "mass political violence." "Mass" denotes activity engaged in by large groups rather than individuals acting alone; "political" suggests a relationship between such activity and competition among domestic groups for power, property and prestige; and "violence" is narrowly construed as resulting in physical damage to persons or property. In short, the materials reproduced herein are intended to illuminate the resort to violence by American groups seeking to change or to preserve the status quo. Although historical, they are of interest to any who wishes to understand the causes, nature and direction of domestic political violence, whether they be social scientists, historians or just interested Americans.

Of course, we are particularly hopeful that these volumes will prove useful to those now engaged in curriculum-revision and the teaching of high school and college courses in the area of American studies. What Christopher Jencks and David Reisman term "the Academic Revolution" has made difficult demands on all educators, not the least of which is the demand for courses which are both relevant to the condition of modern America and of the highest academic quality. These volumes are meant to provide raw material for such courses— primary source matter which will help both instructors and students to deepen and enrich their views of the American experience.

Most important, the editors and publisher recognize that these volumes appear during a national crisis which is also a crisis of the spirit, a time in which the public response to various manifestations of civil disorder is increasingly governed by anger, fear and hysteria. In such an atmosphere it is important to recognize that one is not alone in time—that such events have taken place before in America and, unless fundamental changes in our social and political life take place, will probably recur in the future. Our fondest hope is that this work, and others like it, will help to keep alive, in a time of growing unreason, the spirit of reasoned inquiry.

RICHARD E. RUBENSTEIN
The Adlai Stevenson Institute
Chicago, Illinois

ROBERT M. FOGELSON
Harvard-MIT Joint Center
for Urban Studies
Cambridge, Massachusetts

ILLEGAL PRACTICES

OF THE DEPARTMENT OF JUSTICE

TO THE AMERICAN PEOPLE

REPORT

UPON THE

ILLEGAL PRACTICES

OF THE

UNITED STATES DEPARTMENT OF JUSTICE

R. G. Brown,
Memphis, Tenn.

Zechariah Chafee, Jr.,
Cambridge, Mass.

Felix Frankfurter,
Cambridge, Mass.

Ernst Freund,
Chicago, Ill.

Swinburne Hale,
New York City.

Francis Fisher Kane,
Philadelphia, Pa.

Alfred S. Niles,
Baltimore, Md.

Roscoe Pound,
Cambridge, Mass.

Jackson H. Ralston,
Washington, D. C.

David Wallerstein,
Philadelphia, Pa.

Frank P. Walsh,
New York City.

Tyrrell Williams,
St. Louis, Mo.

NATIONAL POPULAR GOVERNMENT LEAGUE

WASHINGTON, D. C.

MAY, 1920

TO THE AMERICAN PEOPLE:

For more than six months we, the undersigned lawyers, whose sworn duty it is to uphold the Constitution and Laws of the United States, have seen with growing apprehension the continued violation of that Constitution and breaking of those Laws by the Department of Justice of the United States government.

Under the guise of a campaign for the suppression of radical activities, the office of the Attorney General, acting by its local agents throughout the country, and giving express instructions from Washington, has committed continual illegal acts. Wholesale arrests both of aliens and citizens have been made without warrant or any process of law; men and women have been jailed and held *incomunicado* without access of friends or counsel; homes have been entered without search-warrant and property seized and removed; other property has been wantonly destroyed; workingmen and workingwomen suspected of radical views have been shamefully abused and maltreated. Agents of the Department of Justice have been introduced into radical organizations for the purpose of informing upon their members or inciting them to activities; these agents have even been instructed from Washington to arrange meetings upon certain dates for the express object of facilitating wholesale raids and arrests. In support of these illegal acts, and to create sentiment in its favor, the Department of Justice has also constituted itself a propaganda bureau, and has sent to newspapers and magazines of this country quantities of material designed to excite public opinion against radicals, all at the expense of the government and outside the scope of the Attorney General's duties.

We make no argument in favor of any radical doctrine as such, whether Socialist, Communist or Anarchist. No one of us belongs to any of these schools of thought. Nor do we now raise any question as to the Constitutional protection of free speech and a free press. We are concerned solely with bringing to the attention of the American people the utterly illegal acts which have been committed by those charged with the highest duty of enforcing the laws—acts which have caused widespread suffering and unrest, have struck at the foundation of American free institutions, and have brought the name of our country into disrepute.

These acts may be grouped under the following heads:

(1) *Cruel and Unusual Punishments:*

The Eighth Amendment to the United States Constitution provides:

> "Excessive bail shall not be required nor excessive fines imposed, nor cruel and unusual punishments inflicted."

Punishments of the utmost cruelty, and heretofore unthinkable in America, have become usual. Great numbers of persons arrested, both aliens and citizens, have been threatened, beaten with blackjacks, struck with fists, jailed under abominable conditions, or actually tortured. Annexed hereto as Exhibits 1-1c, 2-2f, 5a, 5b, and 9 are affidavits and evidence of these practices.

(2) *Arrests without Warrant:*

The Fourth Amendment to the Constitution provides:

> "The right of the people to be secure in their persons, houses, papers, and effects, against unreasonable searches and seizures, shall not be violated, and no Warrants shall issue, but upon probable cause, supported by Oath or affirmation, and particularly describing the place to be searched, and the persons or things to be seized."

Many hundreds of citizens and aliens alike have been arrested in wholesale raids, without warrants or pretense of warrants. They have then either been released, or have been detained in police stations or jails for indefinite lengths of time while warrants were being applied for. This practice of making mass raids and mass arrests without warrant has resulted directly from the instructions, both written and oral, issued by the Department of Justice at Washington. The cases are far too numerous to catalogue, but typical instances may be found in Exhibits 1-1b, 2-2f, 5 and 13. The secret instructions of the Department also appear as Exhibits 11 and 12.

(3) *Unreasonable Searches and Seizures:*

The Fourth Amendment has been quoted above.

In countless cases agents of the Department of Justice have entered the homes, offices, or gathering places of persons suspected of radical affiliations, and, without pretense of any search warrant, have seized and removed property belonging to them for use by the Department of Justice. In many of these raids property which could not be removed or was not useful to the Department, was intentionally smashed and destroyed. Exhibit 2a is a photograph of the interior of a house raided by the Department of Justice. Exhibit 14 gives a recent opinion of the U. S. Supreme Court in a non-radical case, condemning seizure without warrant by the Department of Justice, and Exhibit 15 the opinion of the U. S. District Court in Montana in a more flagrant radical case. Other Exhibits bearing on this point are 2, 2a, 3 and 13.

(4) *Provocative Agents:*

We do not question the right of the Department of Justice to use its agents in the Bureau of Investigation to ascertain when the law is being violated. But the American people has never tolerated the use of undercover provocative agents or "agents provocateurs," such as have been familiar in old Russia or Spain. Such agents have been introduced by the Department of Justice into the radical movements, have reached positions of influence therein, have occupied themselves with informing upon or instigating acts which might be declared criminal, and at the express direction of Washington have brought about meetings of radicals in order to make possible wholesale arrests at such meetings. Attention is specially called to Exhibits 10 and 11, which are the secret instructions issued from Washington, Exhibit 13 containing an abstract of the testimony in the Colyer case in this regard, and to Exhibits 6, 7 and 8.

(5) *Compelling Persons to be Witnesses against Themselves:*

The Fifth Amendment provides·as follows:

> "No person   *   *   *   shall be compelled in any criminal case to be a witness against himself, nor be deprived of life, liberty, or property, without due process of law."

It has been the practice of the Department of Justice and its agents, after making illegal arrests without warrant, to question the accused person and to force admissions from him by terrorism, which admissions were subsequently to be used against him in deportation proceedings. Instances of this sort appear in various Exhibits numbers 1, 1b, and 2b-2f. Attention is also called to the Cannone case, Exhibit 9, in which Department agents committed assault, forgery and perjury.

(6) *Propaganda by the Department of Justice:*

The legal functions of the Attorney General are: to advise the Government on questions of law, and to prosecute persons who have violated federal statutes. For the Attorney General to go into the field of propaganda against radicals is a deliberate misuse of his office and a deliberate squandering of funds entrusted to him by Congress. Annexed as Exhibit 17 is a copy of a form letter sent out by the Attorney General under date of January 27, 1920, to many magazines and editors throughout the country, deliberately intended to prejudice them in favor of his actions. Exhibit 18 is a description of an illustrated page offered free to country newspapers at the expense of the Department of Justice, patently designed to affect public opinion in advance of court decision and prepared in the manner of an advertising campaign in favor of repression. These documents speak for themselves.

The Exhibits attached are only a small part of the evidence which may be presented of the continued violation of law by the Attorney General's Department. These Exhibits are, to the best of our knowledge and belief (based upon careful investigation) truthful both in substance and detail. Drawn mainly from the four centers of New York City, Boston, Mass., Detroit, Mich., and Hartford, Conn., we know them to be typical of conditions which have prevailed in many parts of the country.

Since these illegal acts have been committed by the highest legal powers in the United States, there is no final appeal from them except to the conscience and condemnation of the American people. American institutions have not in fact been protected by the Attorney General's ruthless suppression. On the contrary those institutions have been seriously undermined, and revolutionary unrest has been vastly intensified. No organizations of radicals acting through propaganda over the last six months could have created as much revolutionary sentiment in America as has been created by the acts of the Department of Justice itself.

Even were one to admit that there existed any serious "Red menace" before the Attorney General started his "unflinching war" against it, his campaign has been singularly fruitless. Out of the many thousands suspected by the Attorney General (he had already listed 60,000 by name and history on Nov. 14, 1919, aliens and citizens) what do the figures show of net results? Prior to January 1, 1920, there were actually deported 263 persons.

Since January 1 there have been actually deported 18 persons. Since January 1 there have been ordered deported an additional 529 persons, and warrants for 1,547 have been cancelled (after full hearings and consideration of the evidence) by Assistant Secretary of Labor Louis F. Post, to whose courageous reëstablishment of American Constitutional Law in deportation proceedings (see Exhibit 16) are due the attacks that have been made upon him. The Attorney General has consequently got rid of 810 alien suspects, which, on his own showing, leaves him at least 59,160 persons (aliens and citizens) still to cope with.

It has always been the proud boast of America that this is a government of laws and not of men. Our Constitution and laws have been based on the simple elements of human nature. Free men cannot be driven and repressed; they must be led. Free men respect justice and follow truth, but arbitrary power they will oppose until the end of time. There is no danger of revolution so great as that created by suppression, by ruthlessness, and by deliberate violation of the simple rules of American law and American decency.

It is a fallacy to suppose that, any more than in the past, any servant of the people can safely arrogate to himself unlimited authority. To proceed upon such a supposition is to deny the fundamental American theory of the consent of the governed. Here is no question of a vague and threatened menace, but a present assault upon the most sacred principles of our Constitutional liberty.

The foregoing report has been prepared May, 1920, under the auspices of the National Popular Government League.

> R. G. BROWN,
>> Memphis, Tenn.
>
> ZECHARIAH CHAFEE, JR.,
>> Cambridge, Mass.
>
> FELIX FRANKFURTER,
>> Cambridge, Mass.
>
> ERNST FREUND,
>> Chicago, Ill.
>
> SWINBURNE HALE,
>> New York City.
>
> FRANCIS FISHER KANE,
>> Philadelphia, Pa.
>
> ALFRED S. NILES,
>> Baltimore, Md.
>
> ROSCOE POUND,
>> Cambridge, Mass.
>
> JACKSON H. RALSTON,
>> Washington, D. C.
>
> DAVID WALLERSTEIN,
>> Philadelphia, Pa.
>
> FRANK P. WALSH,
>> New York City.
>
> TYRRELL WILLIAMS,
>> St. Louis, Mo.

LIST OF EXHIBITS.

(Italics in these Exhibits are ours.)

EXHIBIT 1.

HARTFORD JAIL SITUATION.

In Bridgeport, Conn., on November 8, 1919, various workingmen had come together to discuss ways and means for buying an automobile to be employed for instruction purposes. The meeting was raided and 63 men arrested without warrants by agents of the Department of Justice and taken to the police station. A day or two later, 16 of these were released. The remaining 47, after being held three days in the police station, where they slept on iron bunks without cover or mattress, and where they were fed little or nothing, were transferred by the Department of Justice to the Hartford jail. Other persons who were arrested in this way or who had applied at the Hartford jail for permission to see their friends, were also taken up and confined in the jail. There were finally 97 men held for deportation. Most of them were questioned by Department of Justice agents; some were beaten or threatened with hanging or suffocation in order to obtain answers from them. Warrants of arrest for these men were requested and obtained from the Department of Labor by the Department of Justice. Most of the 97 prisoners remained in practically solitary confinement until the end of April—five months. When the facts finally came to the attention of Mr. Louis F. Post, Assistant Secretary of Labor, he ordered the men all transferred to the Immigrant Station at Deer Island, Boston.

During these five months the prisoners were allowed no reading matter; were kept alone in their cells except for occasional visits from Department of Justice agents or hearings before Department of Labor Inspectors; were refused, in some cases, knowledge of the charges against them; were refused, in some cases, knowledge of the amount of bail under which they were held; were allowed only 2 to 5 minutes a day to wash their face and hands at a sink outside their cells, and 5 minutes once a month to wash their bodies in a tub, were given practically no exercise, and were fed with foul and insufficient food.

In the Hartford jail there exist four punishment rooms, all alike, unventilated and utterly dark, size 4 feet 3 inches by 8 feet 10 inches, with solid concrete floors, no furniture of any kind, and placed over the pump room of the boiler so that the temperature in them becomes unbearably high. A number of the supposed anarchist or Communist prisoners, probably ten to fifteen, were confined in these rooms for periods of 36 to 60 hours. During their imprisonment in the suffocating heat without air, they were given one glass of water and one slice of bread every 12 hours. Some of them on being released had to be revived before they could be carried to their cells; one man who was in only 36 hours was able to get to his cell unaided.

These Hartford prisoners were practically buried alive for five months, being even denied the privilege of seeing their relatives or friends, who made constant attempts to communicate with them.

Only after a lawyer had finally succeeded in gaining access to the jail, were the conditions at all ameliorated and the men ultimately moved to Deer Island. That there were no substantial charges against at least ten of them is shown by the fact that after being held in $10,000 bail for two months and a half, those ten were released without bail on January 24th. It seems probable that at least a majority had no political views of any special nature, but were simply workingmen of Russian nationality speaking little or no English.

The foregoing statement, with many details, is evidenced by the statements of Isaac Shorr of the New York bar, who represented these men, of an impartial expert investigator who was sent to the jail, and personal interviews with some of the men. Affidavits by some of them follow:

EXHIBIT 1a.

State of Connecticut,
    City of Bridgeport, ss:

SEMEON NAKHWAT, being duly sworn, deposes and says:
I was born in Grodno, Russia, and am thirty-three years old and unmarried.

In the autumn of 1919 I was a member of the Union of Russian Workers. I am not an anarchist, Socialist or Bolshevik and do not take much interest in political theories. I joined the Russian Workers because I was a workman speaking Russian and wanted to associate with other Russians and have the benefit of the social intercourse and instruction in mechanics which the society gave. By trade I am a machinist.

On November 8, 1919, I was at a meeting of Russians in Bridgeport, who had come together to discuss ways and means for buying an automobile to be used for instruction purposes. At that time I was employed by the American Brass Co. in Ansonia as a machinist, working a ten hour day at 46½ cents an hour. At the meeting I speak of, I was arrested with all the other men at the meeting, 63 in number. The arrest was made by Edward J. Hickey, a special agent of the Department of Justice, who had helping him about fourteen Bridgeport policemen in uniform and about nine Department of Justice agents in plain clothes. No warrant of arrest was shown me then or at any other time, nor did I see any warrant shown to anyone else who was arrested.

I was taken with the other men to the police station on Fairfield Avenue and held there three days, being in a cell with two other men. During these three days no one gave me any hearing or asked me any questions. I was then taken to Hartford, Conn., with about forty-eight of the men, being informed that the rest of those arrested had been released.

I was held in the Hartford Jail for six weeks without any hearing. In the seventh week I had one hearing before the Labor Department, which hearing was held in the Post Office Building and was then returned to jail.

In the thirteenth week of my confinement Edward J. Hickey came into my cell and asked me to give him the address of a man called Boyko in Greenpoint, Brooklyn. I did not know this man and told Hickey that I did not. Hickey thereupon struck me twice with his fist, once in the forehead and once in the jaw, whereupon I fell. He then kicked me and I became unconscious. Hickey is a big man, weighing two hundred pounds. For three weeks after this I suffered severe pain where I was kicked in the back.

In the last part of January or early in February, my finger was severely infected. I asked the guards to let me have a doctor to treat my finger. They refused, and I asked again, whereupon they said to come with them. They took me to a room in the basement of the jail with a cement floor, cement walls and an iron door. The room was pitch dark, and the only means for lighting or ventilating it that I could see was a small hole in the door. The floor of this room was hot and the walls were very warm to the touch. I stayed in this room for thirty-six hours, from 8.30 one morning to 8.30 the following evening. At times the room was so hot that I was forced to remove all my clothing except my underwear; at other times I found it necessary to resume my clothing. The evening of the first day I was given one glass of water and one slice of bread, and the morning of the second day I was given the same. I received no other food or water during the thirty-six hours. There was no furniture in the room, and no sanitary facilities except an iron pail. On my release from this room I was barely able to move. No medical attention was provided for my infected finger which did not heal entirely until some time after my release from jail in April.

I was released from the Hartford Jail on April 7th, having been in confinement five months, my release coming about through an attorney who came to the jail to see other prisoners and who, after seeing me, obtained a reduction of my bail from ten thousand dollars to one thousand dollars, and secured the putting up of $1,000 bail. During the five months of my confinement I was continually in my cell the whole time, except that twice during the five months the guards took me out of the cell and tried to force me to run, which I was physically unable to do. During the whole period I had only one interview with a friend, although after my release I learned that seven attempts to see me had been made. The only other times I was out of my cell were for two or three minutes each day when I was allowed to go to wash my face at a sink, and five minutes once a month when I was allowed to take a bath in a tub. Only five minutes were allowed for undressing and taking the bath for each man, and I was forced to go back to my cell without time to get the soap out of my hair. I was not allowed to bathe my body more than once a month in this manner.

The food in the jail was very bad, some of it so foul that it could not be eaten at all and not sufficient in quantity to maintain a person in health.

No books or newspapers were allowed me during the five months, although I asked for them.

During the five months' confinement I was kept alone in a small cell with no one to talk to.

At the time of my arrest I was earning an average of $31.00 per week, including bonus and overtime. Since my release on the 7th day of April I have been unable to secure employment, being informed wherever I apply and state my record that persons under suspicion of being bolsheviks are not desired. I have made diligent effort to obtain employment but have been unable to do so.

SEMEON NAKHWAT.

Witness:
    A. MANKO.

STATE OF CONNECTICUT,
    County of Fairfield,
        City of Bridgeport:

Subscribed and sworn to before me this 18th day of May, 1920.
  [NOTARIAL SEAL.]   JOSEPH L. KOCHISS,
                                           Notary Public.

EXHIBIT 1b.

STATE OF CONNECTICUT,
    City of Bridgeport, ss:

PETER MUSEK, being duly sworn, says:
I reside at No. 437 Helen Street, Bridgeport, Conn. I am 33 years of age and am working as a tailor in Bridgeport. On the 24th day of December, 1919, I left Bridgeport for Hartford and applied for a pass to see a friend, Mike Lozuk, who was arrested on the 8th day of November, 1919, at a meeting place of Russians in Bridgeport. I heard that Lozuk was confined in the Hartford Jail and wanted to see me. As soon as I appeared in the U. S. Post Office Building at Hartford, Conn., where I asked for a pass to see Lozuk, I was searched and immediately put under arrest and questioned by an agent of the Department of Justice. Six men, I presume agents of the Department of Justice, questioned me and threatened to hang me if I do not tell them the truth. In one instance, an agent of the Department of Justice, whose name I do not know, brought a rope and tied it around my neck, stating that he will hang me immediately if I do not tell him who conducts the

meetings and who are the main workers in an organization called the Union of Russian Workers. This inquisition lasted fully three hours, after which I was again threatened to be put into a gas-room and suffocated unless I gave more particulars about other men in the Union of Russian Workers. This was all done in the U. S. Post Office Building in the presence of six agents of the Department of Justice.

From the Post Office Building I was taken to a police station in Hartford, where I was placed in a cell and released about eleven o'clock A. M. on the 26th day of December and taken to the U. S. Post Office Building, where I was again questioned by about five agents of the Department of Justice up to five o'clock in the afternoon. A statement was prepared by these agents in English, which I was ordered to sign. After this I was taken to jail, where I was kept for fully two weeks without any hearings. No visitors were allowed to see me. I was not permitted to write any letters. At the end of about two weeks I was chained to another man and led through the streets of Hartford from the jail to the Department of Justice, where I was questioned by an immigration inspector. At the end of the hearing I was informed that if I wish to be released I will have to put up $10,000 bail. Then I was taken back to the jail, where I remained continually up to and including the 18th day of March, 1920, when I was released on bail.

During my confinement I was given an opportunity to write two letters, was not permitted to have any reading matter and was not given any writing paper, so that I remained in the cell all this time without an opportunity to even see a newspaper or see a friend, with the exception of three visits granted to my sister, who made numerous attempts to see me. My cell was always locked with the exception of two or three minutes a day, when I was permitted to run to a sink and wash my face. I was not even permitted to speak to my neighbor in the next cell, even though I could not see him because of an intervening wall. I was hungry during all the time of my confinement, for it was impossible to eat the food that was supplied by the jail, and I was not permitted to buy anything with my own money. On four or five occasions my sister brought some food, which was delivered to the office and then delivered to me by the jailer. This food assisted materially, and if not for that I would probably have starved.

On the 6th day of February, 1920, a few minutes after Anton Dimitroff was taken to the cellar, I was taken out from my cell and also brought to the basement of the jail and put into a cell high enough for me to stand up in and long enough for me to make about two and a half paces. When I was put in the cell, I heard the jailer say to somebody "Give this man heat." When I came into the cell it was quite warm. Soon thereafter the floor became hot and I nearly roasted. I took my clothes off and remained absolutely naked but the heat was unbearable. About five o'clock a man brought a glass of cold water and one piece of bread. The cold water revived me a little and I heard the man say again, "Give him some more heat." After this the cell became even hotter. I could not stand on my feet any longer and I remained on the floor up to 8 o'clock in the morning, when the door opened and a man handed me a glass of water and threw a piece of bread into the cell. I asked him to bring a doctor for I felt that I was going to die. But he laughed at me, stating that I was strong enough to hold out, and locked the door again. I could not eat the bread that was thrown into my cell that morning, for I felt terrible pain in my chest and half of my body was almost roasted from contact with the hot floor. I remained in the cell up to about 8 o'clock of the night of February 8, 1920. The cell was so dark I could not even see my own hands.

At about eight P. M. on the 8th day of February I heard a voice ordering me to get out, but I was unable to get up. Two men stepped into the cell, lifted me, carried me out of the cell, put my clothes on me, gave me a little cold water, washed my face with cold water, took me out in the hall and a fresh breeze revived me. After which I was taken back to my cell, where I remained to the 18th day of March, 1920, when a number of my friends, among them also a priest, decided that in order to save my life it is necessary to make a collection for bail in the sum of $2,500, which was deposited in Liberty Bonds, and I was released.

When I was arrested, the agents of the Department of Justice took a watch, a pencil, a memorandum book, a belt and several other things from my pocket. They also took an arithmetic, a book on electricity and several other text-books. When I was released I asked for my property, but was told that nobody knows what became of it.

PETER MUZEK.

Witness:
 A. MANKO.

Sworn to before me this 18th day of May, 1920.

State of Connecticut,
  County of Fairfield,
    City of Bridgeport:

Personally appeared Peter Muzek who signed this foregoing instrument to be truth before me this 18th day of May, 1920.

[NOTARIAL SEAL.]   JOSEPH KALAFUS,
                 Notary Public.

EXHIBIT 1c.

State of Connecticut,
  City of Bridgeport, ss:

ANTON DIMITROFF being duly sworn, says:
I am 27 years of age and reside at 732 Hallet Street, Bridgeport, Conn. Prior to November 7, 1919, I owned a barber shop at the same address. On the 7th day of November while in the process of shaving a customer, a few plain-clothes men came in and ordered me to follow them. I was compelled to leave my customer half shaved and despite my request was forced to go with the plain-clothes men without being afforded an opportunity to obtain an overcoat or extra clothes and without being permitted to leave the premises in secure condition. I landed in the police station on Fairfield Avenue, where I was locked in a cell without any food.

I was confined in the police station for 5 days during which time I was not allowed to wash even my hands and face. My assistant who desired to obtain instructions as to the care of my barber shop was refused permission to see me.

On the twelfth day of November, about 10 in the morning I was chained and taken to the Hartford jail. I remained in a cell in that jail from November 12, 1919, to April 7, 1920, a period of almost five months. During the greater part of that time my bail was set at ten thousand dollars, a sum which I was entirely unable to raise. Shortly before my release the bail was reduced to one thousand dollars, the amount in which I was then released.

During the five months of my imprisonment I remained in the cell continually with nothing to read, with no recreation of any kind. I was permitted to wash myself every day but was never given more than five minutes to do so. I never had time to wipe my face or hands and was hurried back, sometimes with the soap still on my head and face. One time I protested and asked for an additional minute or two to wipe my face, but received an answer "Stop barking." In the month of February they permitted me to walk for about ten or fifteen minutes a day. During the time of my confinement I was permitted to see one visitor, although I know that a woman whom I knew came to see me twice and a man came to see me once but was not permitted to do so. I was permitted to write four letters.

About the 6th day of February, 1920, an employee in the jail came and ordered me to carry out the pails from cells. I refused to do that, stating that I was a barber and was ready to work at my trade and that I was ready to carry out my own pail but that I did not intend to carry out pails for other prisoners. I was immediately taken down to the basement and brought into a dark room with no windows and no means of ventilation. As far as I could judge, the size of the room was approximately 8 feet by 4 feet. The floor was of cement and was very hot; even the walls and the door were hot. I was placed in that room at nine o'clock in the morning of February 6, and remained there until two o'clock in the afternoon of February 8, a total of fifty-three hours. The only food that I received while in the cell was one glass of water and a small piece of bread twice a day. I suffered intensely throughout the period of my confinement in that cell, being forced soon after

I was placed therein to remove all my clothing and to remain naked on account of the intense heat. Beginning with the second morning of my confinement, namely the morning of February 7, I was too weak to stand up and remained in a reclining position until I was removed from the cell. My complaints were disregarded until the afternoon of February 8, when my condition was such that I was unable to walk as much as ten feet without stopping several times on account of weakness, dizziness, etc. My left arm and left leg felt paralyzed so that I had difficulty in using them, and the pain in my right leg was intense.

I received medical treatment in the jail immediately after my release from the cell and soon after my release from jail was forced to obtain medical treatment again. For the last three weeks I have been in the hospital, with what I am informed is a form of rheumatism of the nerves, an ailment from which I have never suffered in my life before. I am confined to my bed at frequent intervals and still suffer great pain as a result of my treatment in the jail.

I was forced to sell my barber shop with its entire equipment at a great loss, and am now without a place of business, without tools or the means of purchasing them and in such bad health that I do not know when I shall be able to resume my work in any capacity at all.

ANTON DIMITROFF.

Witness:
ALEX. YARSHOFF,
148 *Bond Street, Bridgeport, Conn.*

State of Connecticut,
County of Fairfield,
City of Bridgeport:

Subscribed and sworn to before me this 18th day of May, 1920.
[notarial seal.] JAMES T. ROURKE,
Notary Public.

Note.—The hot cells in which these men and others were punished became known as the "Steam Room." A belief grew up among the prisoners that in some way steam could be turned on and off at will. We have found no apparatus for such a purpose, and ascribe the belief (1) to excessive unventilated heat which might produce the effect of steam from perspiration, (2) to delirium and alternate fever and chills of men so confined for many hours,—see Nakhwat, top p. 13. (3) to the apparent desire of the guards to stimulate the mental torture of such a belief,—see Musek, third par., p. 14.

EXHIBIT 2.

RAID ON RUSSIAN PEOPLE'S HOUSE.

On November 7, 1919, the most violent of six raids, by agents of the Department of Justice and the New York Bomb Squad, was made upon the Russian People's House, 133 East 15th Street, New York City, in search of supposed anarchists and anarchistic literature.

The executive committee of the Federated Unions of Russian Workers occupied an office in the building, which was confined to one room. The other rooms were used principally as educational classrooms, except a small restaurant or cafeteria.

At the time of the raid the Department agents had a few warrants for the arrest of supposed offenders. They went through the building and broke up and destroyed most of the furniture in the place, including desks and typewriting machines. They "beat up" the persons in the place, amounting to several hundred, with blackjacks and stair rails; broke up all the classes then in session and

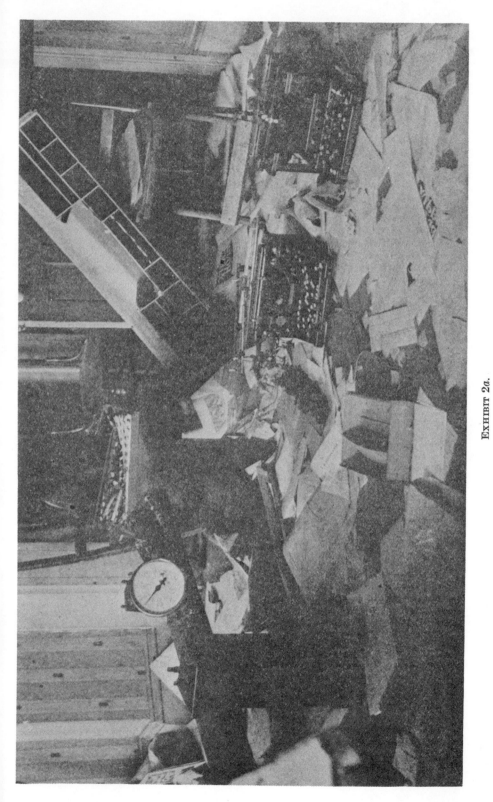

EXHIBIT 2a.

Russian People's House after Raid by Dept. of Justice Agents.

herded the students to the stairways, beating them as they went, shoving them from the landing on to the stairway so that many fell and rolled down the stairs and were trampled upon by those who were shoved after them.

After this raid several hundred prisoners were taken to the office of the Department of Justice at 13 Park Row and there put through the third degree of inquisition. Less than one-fifth of them were held for deportation charges and all the remainder were released to go about their business as being innocent of any wrongdoing.

Many of the persons assaulted suffered serious wounds, and one man who was taken to Ellis Island was in a terrible condition. The manner in which these acts were committed caused a mass meeting of protest to be held the following evening (November 8) at Madison Square Garden, presided over by Dudley Field Malone.

All these facts were immediately put before the Attorney General in detail, in a respectful letter written to him by Isaac Shorr, of the New York bar, on behalf of the persons so arrested. Mr. Shorr asked to be informed whether the acts of the Department's agents had been committed by the authority of the Department, and, if not, that the Department institute an investigation to fix the responsibility.

No answer was ever made to this letter, nor was its receipt acknowledged.

EXHIBIT 2b.

CITY OF NEW YORK,
 County of New York,
  State of New York, ss:

MITCHEL LAVROWSKY, being duly sworn deposes and says: I am fifty years old; am married and have two children; I reside at #999 Southern Boulevard, Borough of Bronx, City of New York; I am a professional teacher and was Principal and teacher in a Russian High School known as Iglitsky High School for fifteen years in the City of Odessa, Russia; I declared my intention to become a citizen of the United States.

On the 7th day of November, 1919, I conducted a class in Russian at 133 East 15th Street, in the Borough of Manhattan, City of New York. At about 8:00 o'clock in the evening, while I was teaching algebra and Russian, an agent of the Department of Justice opened the door of the school, walked in with a revolver in his hands and ordered everybody in the school to step aside; then ordered me to step towards him. I wear eye-glasses and the agent of the Department of Justice ordered me to take them off. Then without any provocation, struck me on the head and simultaneously two others struck and beat me brutally. After I was beaten and without strength to stand on my feet, I was thrown down stairs and while I rolled down, other men, I presume also agents of the Department of Justice, beat me with pieces of wood which I later found out were obtained by breaking the banisters. I sustained a fracture of my head, left shoulder, left foot, and right side. Then I was ordered to wash myself and was taken, as I now understand, to 13 Park Row,* Borough of Manhattan, City of New York, where I was examined by various people and released about 12:00 midnight.

 (Signed)   M. LAVROWSKY.

Sworn to before me this 21st day of November, 1919.

 [SEAL.]   (Signed)   MARKUS ROSENBERG,
                Notary Public.

N. Y. Co., No. 66, N. Y. Reg. No. 10066.

---

*Offices of the Department of Justice.

EXHIBIT 2c.

City of New York,
   County of New York,
      State of New York, ss:

NICAOLI MELIKOFF being duly sworn, says: I reside at 342 East 13th Street, in the Borough of Manhattan, City of New York; I was one of the students in a class-room at 133 East 15th Street, on the second floor. While the class was in session, a few detectives came in and ordered everybody to get up and keep quiet, which everybody obeyed. They then searched everyone in the class-room including me. I had Twenty ($20) Dollars in my pocket, in addition to other papers. These $20 including the other papers were taken from me and I never received the money back. We were then ordered to go out of the room. Outside of the class-room there were two detectives standing and everyone that passed out of the room was beaten. I was struck on my head, and being the last one to go out, was attacked by one detective, who knocked me down again, sat on my back, pressing me down to the floor with his knee and bending my body back until blood flowed out of my mouth and nose. I was then taken to a sink where I was ordered to drink some water and was also ordered to wash my face. After this, I was thrown down stairs, where I fell with my head down to the ground floor, after which I was arrested and taken to 13 Park Row, where I was questioned and released.
   (Signed)   NICAOLI MELIKOFF.

Sworn to before me this 21st day of November, 1919.
   [SEAL.]   (Signed)   MARKUS ROSENBERG,
                                                Notary Public.

N. Y. Co. No. 66, N. Y. Reg. No. 10003.

EXHIBIT 2d.

Copy.

City of New York,
   County of New York,
      State of New York, ss:

VARFOLMEY ISCHENKO, being duly sworn, says: I reside at 94 East 7th Street, in the Borough of Manhattan, City of New York; I am 28 years of age. On the 7th day of November, 1919, I was in a class where Russian was taught; about 8:00 o'clock in the evening, while the class was in session, the door opened and a few detectives came in, searched everybody, including me, after which I was struck on the head with a blackjack, and thrown downstairs, from where I was taken to Park Row, where I was questioned and released.
   (Signed)   VARFOLMEY ISCHENKO.

Sworn to before me this 19th day of November, 1919.
   [SEAL.]   (Signed)   MARKUS ROSENBERG,
                                                Notary Public.
N. Y. Co. No. 66, N. Y. Reg. No. 10003.

EXHIBIT 2e.

City of New York,
   County of New York,
      State of New York, ss:

SEMEON E. KRAVCHUCK, being duly sworn, says, I live at 94 East 7th Street, in the Borough of Manhattan, City of New York. I am 31 years old, and am married. On the 7th day of November, 1919, I was on my way to school at 133 East 15th Street; that for no reason, I was stopped by some unknown person and ordered to go into the building, where I was immediately attacked and brutally beaten, as a result of which I received one blow on the head, one tooth was knocked out, and was bruised all over my body, after which I was taken to the Department of Justice where I was questioned and released.

(Signed)   SEMEON E. KRAVCHUCK.

Sworn to before me this 19th day of November, 1919.

[SEAL.]   (Signed)   MARKUS ROSENBERG,
Notary Public.

N. Y. Co. No. 66, N. Y. Reg. No. 10003.

EXHIBIT 2f.

CITY OF NEW YORK,
    County of New York,
        State of New York, ss:

PETER KARAS, being duly sworn, says: I reside at #624 East 11th Street, in the Borough of Manhattan, City of New York; on the 7th day of November, 1919, about 8:00 P. M., I was on 15th Street, between 3rd Avenue and Irving Place; without any notice to me, two men which I afterward found out, were agents of the Department of Justice, attacked me, struck me on the face, and beat me up otherwise, brutally, after which I was taken to 13 Park Row, New York City, where I was examined by men whom I do not know, and then released.

(Signed)   PETER KARAS.

Sworn to before me this 19th Day of November, 1919.

[SEAL.]   (Signed)   MARKUS ROSENBERG,
Notary Public.

N. Y. Co. No. 66, N. Y. Reg. No. 10003.

Note: To the same general effect is the testimony of man after man examined in the deportation proceedings that grew out of the various raids on the Russian People's House.

EXHIBIT 3.

STATE OF NEW YORK,
    County of New York, ss:

ALBERT DE SILVER, being duly sworn, deposes and says:

That on the 6th day of January, 1920, I was informed that a raid was in progress at the office of "Novy Mir," a Russian newspaper, then published at No. 113 East 10th Street, New York City. Upon receiving this information, I at once went to said premises occupied by the Novy Mir, and when I arrived found a police patrol drawn up outside, into which a number of police officers and a number of men in plain clothes were carrying boxes, filled with books and papers. I recognized and spoke to Mr. Mortimer R. Davis, special agent of the Bureau of Investigations of the United States Department of Justice, who seemed to be in charge. I inquired of Mr. Davis, with whom I was acquainted, whether I might go inside, and he said that he didn't care but that I might get hit over the head if I did. When the patrol wagon had left I went in and knocked on the door of the front room, first floor. The premises were in charge of one uniformed policeman who admitted me to the first floor which had formerly been occupied as the editorial offices of the paper. The two rooms on that floor were in great confusion, the floors being entirely covered with torn books and papers, some of them in Russian and some of them in English. Many books had been destroyed by being ripped down the back. I saw among them a number of recent books on Russian conditions such as are sold in all book stores and including "The Red Heart of Russia" by Bessie Beattie, "Ten Days That Shook the World" by John Reed and others. Pieces of broken typewriters were mixed up in the wreckage; two desks had been drawn across the front windows so as to block the view from the outside; other desks and tables were upset and the contents removed and torn, the drawers lying about the room, and in some cases their panels and drawers smashed.

(Sgd.) ALBERT DE SILVER.

Sworn to before me this 28th day of April, 1920.

J. W. MIDDLEBROOK,
Notary Public, New York County.

N. Y. Co. Clk.'s No. 142, N. Y. Reg. No. 2202.
My commission expires March 30, 1922.

EXHIBIT 4.

SALSEDO AND ELIA CASES.

At about 4 A. M. on the morning of Monday, May 3rd, Andrea Salsedo jumped or fell from the 14th story window of the Department of Justice in the Park Row building, New York City, where he had been secretly confined for about eight weeks.

His death makes it impossible to ascertain all the facts in the cases of himself and Roberto Elia, who was confined with him. The main facts so far known are as follows:

At the request of the Department of Justice, a deportation warrant was issued by the Department of Labor against Elia on February 26, and a similar warrant against Salsedo on March 10, 1920. These warrants were in the usual form, commanding that the men be taken into the custody of the Department of Labor. Some time before March 10, both men were arrested by the Department of Justice, and were thenceforth secretly confined together, without hearing of any kind and without the knowledge of the Department of Labor, by the Department of Justice, in its offices on the 14th floor of the Park Row Building. Two days after Salsedo fell to his death on May 3rd, Elia was given up by the Department of Justice to the Department of Labor and transferred to Ellis Island.

The history of all that may have happened to the men during the eight weeks of their secret confinement will never be known. It is claimed by the Department of Justice that they had turned State's evidence and were confined at their own desire for their own protection.

The foregoing statement rests upon information given by Walter Nelles of the New York Bar, now retained as counsel for Elia in his deportation proceedings, upon the main facts agreed upon in the various newspaper accounts, and upon evidence given by Assistant Secretary Louis F. Post before the Rules Committee of the House of Representatives.

EXHIBIT 5.

JAILING RADICALS IN DETROIT.

By Frederick R. Barkley.

(The Nation, N. Y., Jan 31, 1920, and April 10, 1920.)

On January 2 Arthur L. Barkey, chief agent of the Department of Justice in Detroit, received an order from Attorney General Palmer instructing Mr. Barkey, according to his own statement, to raid the headquarters of a group of interdicted organizations, principally the Communist party, "as long as they continue to meet," in a "supreme effort to break the back of radicalism" in Detroit. As a result, eight hundred men were imprisoned for from three to six days in a dark, windowless, narrow corridor running around the big central areaway of the city's antiquated Federal Building; they slept on the bare stone floor at night. * * * They were compelled to stand in long lines for access to the solitary drinking fountain and the one toilet; they were denied all food for twenty hours, and after that were fed on what their families brought in; and they were refused all communication with relatives or with attorneys. These eight hundred men, so closely packed that they had to step over one another's bodies to move about at all, included in their number citizens and aliens, college graduates and laborers, skilled mechanics making $15 a day and boys not yet out of short trousers. They were seized without warrant while attending dances and classes in physical geography and similar subjects; * * *

The raiders held altogether, it would appear from tabulations of releases made from time to time, more than 350 American citizens, or aliens who could prove conclusively, in the Department's secret examinations, that they had not even a "cursory interest in radicalism." For from three to six days they held these men and boys in this temporary prison, and then began to transfer them to precinct police stations and to the "bull pen" in the Municipal Building. * * *

From 130 to 140 men were herded into the police "bull pen," a room built to hold petty offenders for not more than three or four hours, a one-window cellar room, twenty-four by thirty feet in size, with no place to rest but wooden benches and a stone floor. For seven days these men were held here, sleeping on the floor, fed largely by the contributions from relatives handed through the single grated door. * * *

Today, January 19, the 300 men left of the 800 seized are housed in an old army fort here. In addition, about 140 are out on bond. Warrants for holding these 440 arrived from Washington on January 12, ten days after the raids.

Detroit, March 23.

Three months after their arrest in mass raids conducted by the Department of Justice, 150 Detroit aliens are still held in an old army fort in this city, with no information available from Immigration Bureau officials, who are in charge of them, concerning when or whether they will be deported or freed.

Four hundred and fifty aliens have been confined in this old fort since they were removed there on January 13 from temporary prisons. * * * Of these 450, in round numbers—the Immigration Bureau seems to have no exact figures available—66 have been released for lack of evidence, 120 have been ordered deported, and decisions on the rest are still awaited from Washington. Of the 384 whose cases have not yet been passed on or who have been ordered deported, approximately 240 are out on bail. The rest are held at the fort. * * *

Three weeks ago the 220 men then held sent out an open letter in which they pleaded to be deported immediately with their wives and children. * * *

"The food we get is foul," this letter continues, "and we are kept in cold cells, almost without light. * * * The prison guards treat us brutally, inhumanely. * * * Our helplessness is being exploited by these guards. We are permitted to be taken under guard to stores to make some purchases in preparation for our deportation, and for these privilegese they expect from us bribes." * * *

In the meantime the dependents of many are in a state of apprehension and uncertainty, cared for by a charitable agency which came to their aid only when a committee of prominent Detroit clubwomen had brought their plight to public attention, six weeks after their supporters had been arrested. * * *

EXHIBIT 5a.

STATE OF MICHIGAN,
  County of Wayne, ss:

ALEXANDER BUKOWETSKY, being duly sworn according to law, deposes and says:

On November 8, 1919, I was arrested while attending a concert given by the Union of Russian Workers at the Social Turner Hall, and with thirteen other men was taken to Hunt Street Station.

We were put in cells for ten days, the only food we had being two slices of bread a day, and water. We slept two on a bench, made of wood and about 15″ wide, without blankets, mattresses or pillows. During our confinement we were not allowed to get into communication with any of our relatives, or friends,—they knew nothing of our whereabouts.

At the end of ten days we were taken to the Department of Justice, where we were roughly handled and beaten. Then we were sent to the Wayne County Jail. This was about November 17 or 18, 1919. We remained here until about January 21, 1920. Here we were allowed to receive our relatives and were given fairly good treatment. When we were brought before Jailer Brooks for the first time, he refused to take us in because he stated there was no room. Inspector Dowig suggested our sleeping on the floor but there hardly seemed room enough for this. After this suggestion he told Jailer Brooks that we could stand. We were finally accepted. Then we were compelled to sleep on the floor for over two months. A ward was able to hold 23 people, however, at times there were over one hundred.

At the Wayne County Jail our friends and relatives were also allowed to bring us food.

On January 11, 1920, 33 men were sent to Ellis Island to await deportation. Five of us were sent to Fort Wayne where there were 250 Communists. Treatment here was very bad, especially by Sgts. Taylor and Ross, and other guards. The food was very poor and at times insufficient to care for from ten to forty men. Whenever we made complaints to the guards we were insulted and brutally treated.

During our stay at Fort Wayne some of us were given permission to go downtown to buy things for our deportation to Russia,—we of course were accompanied by guards and were informed that we were not to pay these guards for taking us. However, it is generally known that the guards compelled the men to pay them under threat of punishment when they returned to the Barracks. They accepted money and presents. Many things were purchased for Sgt. Taylor under threat by him,—for instance one man by the name of Morovitz and one other, whose name I can not remember, were made to buy Sgt. Taylor a gold ring costing $7.50, and some other men were compelled to buy him a suit of clothes, and many other things. In the instance of one Mr. Zaitscf he was told by Sgt. Ross that he would have to give $4.00 before he could go home, although the guard who was to take Zaitsch home stated that he did not want the money and that he knew these men needed all they had, but Ross insisted that the money be paid the guard and so it was. Another man gave Ross $8.00 in order that he could go down town. Ross was also given many presents.

After some time elapsed I requested the privilege of interviewing Dr. Prentis, Inspector of Immigration. Sgt. Ross told me that if we stayed there fifteen years and he was there that length of time he would never allow me to see Dr. Prentis. However, Dr. Prentis came to Fort Wayne and I got to talk with him. I explained everything as above relating to him the terrible treatment we had been receiving, the poor food they had been giving us, which was at times insufficient to care for all of us and the bribery that was taking place, and he promised to see that things were better.

Conditions changed for about one week and we were relieved. However, very suddenly the old trouble started again. Visiting periods were limited to ten minutes and at times our relatives and friends were made to stand outside of the gate for half an hour and sometimes an hour at a time in the cold before they were allowed to enter; sometimes, frequently, I should say, they were turned away after waiting nearly an hour, with the remark that they could not see any one.

After Dr. Prentis' visit I was threatened with solitary confinement; was roughly handled and insulted by guards and those in charge. Conditions continued to grow worse until we could stand it no longer and we requested some relief, only to be further threatened with punishment of one form or another. I sent a letter to Dr. Prentis, finally, and this was forwarded to Inspector Brondick, who was instructed by Dr. Prentis, to investigate conditions as represented in my letter. He arrived at Fort Wayne. The first time he visited us he succeeded in showing us that he was helping us. Then for another week conditions were good until he gained our confidence. Right after this the oppression started again and it was as bad if not worse than before. We begged to be deported when we thought we could not stand it any longer, but our demands were only laughed at. At this time we again wrote a note to Insp. Brondick asking him to come in. When he came around he picked up the note, read it, dismissed us (we went away very quietly), then tore the note in many pieces and instead of giving us an answer insulted us by unspeakable words; then went on into the barracks where another plea was waiting for him. He did the same thing with this note,—tore it to pieces. He also instructed his guard to point a pistol at the head of August Harriman, for no reason at all. We had simply asked not to be insulted and to be treated as though we were human.

The next day we were not allowed to see any one and our complaints were not acknowledged. We then went on a hunger strike to enforce our pleas. This lasted for two days. After that time nine men were taken to Pontiac jail. We remained there for a period of nine days. The Sheriff at this institution repeatedly came into the jail with his gun, calling us names, particularly calling me a "Red" and a "Bolshevic," and stating that he would kill us. For two days were not allowed to see our relatives and when they were admitted they were only allowed three minutes. They came with a permit from Dr. Prentis. When these people were allowed to come in they were grabbed by the arms and roughly handled and pushed about. One woman was pushed and she fell to the floor, after which it was necessary to call a Doctor.

We were then taken back to Detroit by Sgt. Ross and Insp. Brondick.

When we were sent to Pontiac they rifled our pockets and took all our personal property including money, refusing at the time to give us a receipt. When we were taken back to Detroit some of our things were returned, however, one Mr. Kosakoff was short $16.50; Mr. Anotski $7.40, Mr. Miller $1.25, and among other things two fountain pens were missing. When this was reported no attention or record was made of it. Our bags were sent to the Detroit Immigration Service Station, and we were taken back to Fort Wayne. When we were taken back we decided not to talk to any of the guards or officials so that they could have no cause for complaint and that we might at least be left alone.

The following day my wife came with my two children, Violet, age 12, and Robert, age 4, with a permit from Dr. Prentis to see me. They allowed them to come into the office. The guard was sent after me to see my family. As soon as I came to the doors of the office, Sgt. Ross who had been standing there with his hands in his pocket and his arms stretched across the front of the door, pushed me back out of the door. With surprise I asked him "What is the matter, I was called by Guardman and when I come you push me out." At the same time my wife and children were pulled out of the room by their arms. I did not have a chance to say one word to them. They were pulled into the hall by Sgt. Mitchell and then he brought my wife close to me and hit her with his fist both on her back and over her breast. My wife and children began to cry, and I asked Sgt. Mitchell what he was trying to do, if he was trying to provoke me so that I would start to fight. Instead of answering me he struck her several times more and made her fall to the floor. With that he grabbed a shot gun and at the same time Ross took a club and then one other guardman, Clark, came in and he too with the butt of his pistol struck me over the head. I fell to the floor with three holes in my head,—I fell with blood streaming all over my body.

My little girl Violet, saw this and ran over to the guardman and with her hand smoothed his face crying "Please don't hurt my father and mother," but with all this, seeing the blood on the floor from my head and my wife and children crying they paid no attention to us.

I thought they would kill me so I called "Comrades, help me," they were upstairs but no one came to help as they could not come down, but at the same time by order of Insp. Brondick they started to shoot at the crowd upstairs without cause and shot one man by the name of Zuba, in the leg, and he is at present in the Receiving Hospital.

I finally got up and ran, breaking through the guards and running into the Barracks. They tried to send me to the hospital but I did not want to go as I thought Dr. Prentis would come in at a time like this. Finally he did come and I asked to have him come to see me, refusing to take medical aid until he came. However, right after this Dr. Prentis called me to the office at the Barracks. He sent a guardman after me, but as I did not know what he wanted I refused to go, thinking they were going to beat me again. I again asked that Dr. Prentis come to the Barracks as he did at other times, to see me, but he did not come. One man then cut off my hair and bandaged my wounds.

At five o'clock they called a patrol and took me with another man by the name of Harriman to the Wayne County Jail.

All of the above trouble started because I told Dr. Prentis the truth, of the briberies going on at Fort Wayne, and the poor treatment we had received.

All suit cases and hand bags were sent here, but most of the things were missing from the bags. From my hand bag I missed a safety razor, shoes valued at $12.00, handkerchiefs, and many other things.

Mr. Harriman's bag had been broken into, the lock removed and things stolen from it. When he reported this to Dr. Prentis some of the things were returned, but not all of his things.

The following day the papers had it that we tried to escape, which was untrue. No one wanted to escape, all we asked was fair treatment and to be deported as soon as possible. But this request was not granted and we had to stand all of the brutality they wished to bestow upon us.

They said too that Mr. Harriman had helped me,—but this was not true as he was in another barracks, and he did not even know that we were having trouble in our barracks, until they came and took him with me to the Wayne County Jail.

I am satisfied with the treatment I am receiving here as they are good to me. The food I do not eat as my friends bring whatever they can. I have a good place to sleep and can have my friends and relatives come to see me.

At the time my wife was notified to get ready to be deported to Russia she had two days in which time to dispose of all our things, among which was a new sewing machine. If she could only have had this she could have made things to sell and would not have had to go to friends and ask them to help her and keep her from the cold and from starving to death with my children. But this was also sold and there was nothing to do but wait. She is now staying with kind friends who have given her a bed and are keeping her and my children warm. For two months however, she was compelled to sleep on the floor on a mattress, because the friends with whom she could stay had no other room.

When I came to America I came with the thought that I was coming to a free country,—a place of freedom and happiness, and I was anxious to come,—to get away from the Czaristic form of Government. As much as I was anxious to come here to America I am a hundred times more anxious to run away from Americanism to return to Soviet Russia, where I will at least be able to live.

For six months I have been confined in jail, the Government refusing to either deport or release me together with my wife and children. They have been left, during this time, without means of support. Had it not been for the kindness of the poor, who are our friends, our women and children would have perished.

The Government has decided that we are to be deported. We ask only that this sentence be carried out that we with our families be deported to Soviet Russia, and that this cruel and inhuman policy of keeping men for six months in jail under sentence of deportation, refusing to either deport or release us, and leaving our families to starve, be ended. We ask only of you that you carry out the sentence which you yourself have decreed,—that we be deported immediately with our families to Soviet, Russia.

I ask this in the name of Justice.

And further deponent says not.

(Signed) ALEXANDER BUKOWETSKY.

Subscribed and sworn to before me this third day of April, A. D. 1920.

(Signed) S. E. GRAMER,
Notary Public.

My commission expires in the County of Wayne, State of Michigan, August 4, 1923.

EXHIBIT 5b.

My name is Violet Bukowetsky. I am twelve years old, and live at 73 Greeley St., Detroit, Mich.

Thursday afternoon, March 18th, my mother, my brother and I went down to Fort Wayne to see my father. We went to the office and sat down on the bench. Brondyke too took the pass and said "Did you come here to make trouble again?" My mother said, "Why no I just came to see my husband." Brondyke said, "If you talk back like that here is your pass, get out, "My mother said, "I won't get out until I see my husband." Then Brondyke started to push my mother out, and he punched her in the back. One of the guards called my father in the hall. When my father came in, one of the guards hit my mother in the chest with a riot gun, which knocked her breath out. Then my father jumped in front of my mother and said, "You have no right to hit my wife like that." When he said that, they started to hit him with sticks and guns, and whatever they had. My mother got frightened and started to holler, and Rouse hit my father on the head with a stick. He called to the comrades to come and help him, but they could not come down. After awhile someone else hit my father on the head with a stick again and he fell down. One of the guards shot three times in the crowd, and shot Zu Zubka in the knee with a bullet. And after that they chased us out.

We went to Dr. Prentiss and my mother could not say anything to Dr. Prentiss, and one of the ladies, Mrs. Mazeika, who had been out to Fort Wayne at the time we were there told Dr. Prentiss all about it. Dr. Prentiss said that he would see about it. Then a doctor was called for my mother and he said her nerves were all broken down. Then we went home and she was sick in bed, has been sick in bed ever since.

The next day, March 19th, I went to the County Jail to see my father and he had three holes in his head and his face was swollen and he was hurt in the neck. Then I went home and told my mother, about it. She was glad to hear that he was living, as she thought that he would be dead.

(Signed)   VIOLET BUKOWETSKY.

Subscribed and sworn to before me this 3rd day of April, 1920.
(Signed)   S. E. GRAMER,
Notary Public, Wayne Co., Mich.

My com. expires Augu. 14, 1923.

EXHIBIT 5c.

STATEMENT AS TO FOREGOING AFFIDAVITS.

The statements in Bukowetsky's affidavit are also vouched for by two representative women of Detroit who have investigated the deportation situation there. Miss Agnes Inglis says (May 5):

"Everything he said was true and more. I didn't see all that happened that he told about in his affidavit. But I saw Zuba's shot leg and Bukowetsky's head, and I know what the guards at the fort are like * * * and have heard and seen the way the visitors were treated, hardly getting in when they had to leave. I could stay in as long as I liked, acting as a sort of lawyer, but after coming long distances and even from out of town, I have seen women put out after being in only a few minutes. The guards are anything but the kind of men they ought to be. One doesn't naturally think highly of county jails, but we have come to think of the one here with almost affection because it is so much better than the fort. One has no fear of cruelty at the jail. One senses terror at the fort.

"Dr. Prentis told me yesterday that Bukowetsky could go out without promising anything or signing anything. All he will be obliged to say is that either he or his wife will report his address once a month so they can be notified when it comes time for them to be deported. * * * The 146 men yet at the fort have refused parole. They say Deport or Release. Bukowetsky says so, too."

Mrs. Louis Danziger says:

"I believe the story of Bukowetsky is true. He has told it to me twice and to others as many times—and always the same. Bukowetsky came to America in 1907, with his wife and infant babe,—Violet; the boy Robert was born here. Dr. Prentis, Immigration Officer in Chicago, offered Bukowetsky a release—on condition that he will report to him either in person or in writing once in two or three weeks. Mr. Bukowetsky will not accept release in this manner—either absolute release or deportation is his stand."

Note: All of the foregoing evidence as to Detroit is generally corroborated by the statement of Solomon G. Paperno, a Detroit lawyer who represented fifty or more of the aliens arrested.

EXHIBIT 6.

CASE OF JULIA PRATT (*re* provocative agents).

Miss Julia Pratt was a teacher of drawing in the public schools of Buffalo. In January, 1920 she was suspended by the Board of Education, and hearings were had before the Board on January 27, and March 16. At the first hearing one Herman Bernhard appeared as witness against Miss Pratt, and testified that he was a secret agent of the Department of Justice; that as such agent he had joined the Communist Party, Buffalo branch, and became Recording Secretary of the branch. He produced the books which he kept as Secretary of the organization and identified the enrollment of Miss Pratt as a member of the Party, and the dates on which she paid her dues. He also testified to other alleged activities of Miss Pratt.

Miss Pratt was dismissed by the Board of Education and her contract with the city cancelled on April 19, 1920 on the ground of her membership in the Communist Party.

A statement made by Miss Pratt April 21, 1920, contains the following:

"On July 18, 1919, Miss Harris invited me to her home to meet some 'interesting intellectual friends of hers,' as she put it. I went out to Kenmore. Herman Bernhard came in with two women friends of his. He constantly injected overdrawn statements against the Government into the conversation, and outlined in glowing terms the work the Communist Party would perform in emancipating the oppressed and exploited. * * * Bernhard later came to my house with others of the same group, ate at my table and I played the harp for him. It is on the testimony of this *agent provocateur* that the Board has dismissed me."

EXHIBIT 7.

CASE OF HENRY PETZOLD (*re* provocative agents).

Henry Petzold, a member of the Communist Labor Party, was convicted before Justice McCarthy in the Hudson County, N. J., Court, in March, 1920, for an alleged infringement of the New Jersey statute which prohibits "inciting * * * or encouraging hostility or opposition to the government of the United States or of the State of New Jersey." Evidence against him was given by two under-cover agents of the Department of Justice. One of them was Herman Bernhard, who also gave evidence in the Julia Pratt case, Exhibit 6, and who testified in the Petzold case that he had been assigned by the Department of Justice to watch the radical movement; became a member of the Communist Party and rose to the position of Recording Secretary of Local Buffalo, that he traveled to other cities as well and had the confidence of radicals in Rochester, Detroit, and other places. It further appeared from Bernhard's testimony that he joined the Socialist Party before the Communist Party was organized. He probably, therefore, belonged to the "Left Wing" and joined in the organization of the Communist Party as a whole at its first convention.

The second government witness, one Cummerow, testified that at the instructions of the Department of Justice he attended the Communist Labor Party Convention held in Chicago from August 30th to September 5th and took a complete memorandum of the proceedings. Petzold, he testified, was a delegate to the Convention and a member of the Constitution Committee.

Judge McCarthy sentenced Petzold to be imprisoned for a term of 3 to 10 years, and then suspended sentence because of his previous record of good character.

EXHIBIT 8.

UNDER-COVER PRIVATE INFORMANTS.

In Western Pennsylvania and West Virginia at least, the following practices exist:

1. Under-cover informants employed by private detective agencies, which in turn are employed by the steel and coal companies, supply to those detective agencies, and through them to the companies and to the Department of Justice, information concerning members of labor organizations.

2. Arrests are frequently made upon the unsupported statements of these under-cover private informants; these arrests are made by local police without warrant and reported to the Department of Justice, which sends its investigator to go through the men arrested and ascertain if there are any extreme radicals among them; and then sets the machinery of the Department of Labor in motion for their deportation.

In other words, the steel and coal companies use the local and Federal governments to harass and get rid of "troublesome" workers.

The foregoing statements rest upon evidence of witnesses (both Immigration officials and officers of "labor detective agencies") examined before a commission sent by the Interchurch World Movement to investigate and report upon the Steel Strike.

Along this line, there is a case in the files of the Labor Department in Washington in which an under-cover informant of a private detective agency operating in Youngstown, Ohio, became secretary of a branch of the Communist Party, was subsequently used by the Department of Justice, was himself taken up in a raid with other persons, was given assurances by the Department of Justice that if deported he would be allowed to return to this country, finally lost his nerve and testified to these facts at his deportation hearing, and is now in the custody of the Department of Labor pending the determination of his case.

EXHIBIT 9.

IN THE MATTER OF GASPARE CANNONE.

STATE OF NEW YORK,
  County of New York, ss:

WALTER NELLES, being duly sworn, says:
I am attorney for Gaspare Cannone. He was taken to Ellis Island on April 2, 1920, under a deportation warrant issued April 1 at the instance of Special Agents of the Department of Justice. Hearings were held at Ellis Island on April 14 and 15, and his case now awaits the decision of the Secretary of Labor.

The following is the substance of Cannone's sworn statements: He was seized at his home in Brooklyn by agents of the Department of Justice about noon on March 30, 1920, *without charge or warrant,* and taken to the office of the Department of Justice in the Park Row Building, New York City. There he was beaten and kicked by a handsome agent in a blue-striped silk shirt, in the presence of three other agents (one—Faulhaber—a stenographer, and one,—Palmera,—an Italian interpreter), who proceeded to interrogate him. They tried to get him to furnish evidence implicating persons named John Berry, Recchi, and Valdinoce (all entirely unknown to him) in the Washington bomb explosions of last year (of which he knew nothing). They continually beset him to "Tell the truth," "stop lying," "come across,"—and then, when he gave truthful answers to their questions, they called him a "damned liar," a "son of a bitch," and many other things of which the opprobrious meaning was clear, but which he knew too little English to understand exactly. He was told that they would be easy with him if he said what they wanted him to. Failing to get anything from him, they told him he would be deported.

He was held by the Department of Justice, and denied communication with anyone outside, from noon on March 30 to noon on April 2, when he was taken to Ellis Island. Each night he was taken to Police Headquarters and locked up in a bare cell without blankets or covering. He was given five meals in the four days.

On his last appearance in the Park Row office, Exhibit B, (a photograph of which is hereto annexed) was put before him, and he was told to sign. He refused, because it was not a correct record of what he had said. Of the inherent likelihood that any free man in his senses would sign such a document, nothing need be said.

A forged signature of "Gaspare Cannone" was subscribed to Exhibit B. Agent Palmera swore, at the hearing at Ellis Island on April 14, 1920, that he had seen this "signature" *written by Cannone.* Comparison is invited between the photograph of this forgery and the photographs of Cannone's genuine signature; Cannone made the ten signatures (Exhibit F) at the hearing on April 15th; he had previously, on his arrival at Ellis Island two weeks earlier, made the other genuine signature (Exhibit G) in answer to the Inspector's question: "What is the correct spelling of your name?"

From his beating on March 30th Cannone retained for upwards of two weeks a conspicuous "black eye." Record of this was preserved in a photograph of him made for the Department of Justice at Police Headquarters on March 31, 1920. When I examined the Inspector's file relative to Cannone at Ellis Island on April 14th, I found in it four prints of this photograph, which I put in evidence at the hearing as Exhibit D. Annexed hereto is a photograph of this Exhibit.

The whole evidence against Cannone was Exhibit B. Advised at the outset of the hearing on April 14th that I would claim to have the deportation warrant vacated by reason of the criminal practices of the Department of Justice on March 30th and 31st in creating the alleged "evidence," Department of Justice Agents Faulhaber and Palmera, who testified on April 14th, determined to set up an alibi for themselves as to March 30th and 31st, and to deny, not that Cannone had been beaten at the Department of Justice, but that he had been beaten *in their presence.* They accordingly insisted that they had never seen Cannone until April 1, *after his arrest under the deportation warrant issued on that date,* and that it was on that date, and not before, that he made *in their presence,* the statements attributed to him in Exhibit B. They overlooked, or perhaps were unaware of the existence of a written statement from their own office fixing the date of Exhibit B as *March 30th*—the day upon which Cannone says he was *beaten* in their presence. In the Inspector's file, attached to Exhibit B, I found what the Inspector stated was the letter of transmittal of Exhibit B from the Department of Justice to Ellis Island. It is as follows:

"Department of Justice.

Bureau of Investigation.

Post Office Box 241.

C. J. S.—J. W. D.

City Hall Station,
New York, April 1, 1920.

Byron H. Uhl, Esq., Acting Commissioner of Immigration, Ellis Island, New York.

Attention Mr. Schell.

DEAR SIR: Attached herewith please find a copy of part of the testimony of Gaspare Cannone, which testimony was taken at the office of Bureau ON THE AFTERNOON OF MARCH 30th.

Very truly yours,

(Signed)

GEORGE F. LAMB,
Division Superintendent."

EXHIBIT E.

Photograph of Cannone as he normally appears for comparison with photograph after "third degree."
Note: This photograph has been obtained since Mr. Nelles' affidavit was made.

EXHIBIT D.

Photograph of photograph of Cannone made March 31, 1920, after two days' "interrogation."

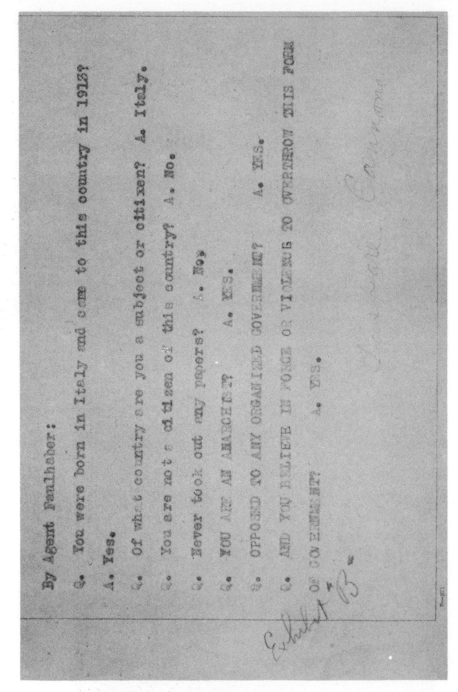

EXHIBIT B.

Alleged statements of Cannone, with forged signature.

Brought to Ellis Island I⟨n⟩ boat Apr. 2/30

Gaspare Cannone

Exhibit G.

Genuine signature made by Cannone on April 3, 1920, in response to Inspector's question, "What is the correct spelling of your name?"

Gaspare Cannone
Gaspare Cannone
Gaspare Cannone
Gaspare Cannone
Gaspare Cannone
Gaspare Cannone
Gaspare Cannone
Gaspare Cannons
Gaspars Cannone
Gaspare Cannons

Exhibit F.

Ten genuine signatures made by Cannone at the hearing on April 14, 1920.

I offered this letter in evidence, and it was received and marked Exhibit H.

A few days after the hearing I saw the Inspector. He told me that this letter, with two others of less importance which had also been received, and his own statement as to its receipt in due course together with Exhibit B, *were no longer part of the official record.*

"I CUT THEM OUT," said the Inspector.

I had fortunately, however, made a long-hand copy of the letter in my note-book during the hearing. * * *

On April 14th, in the presence of Agents Faulhaber and Palmera, Cannone had testified at some length as to his beating at the Department of Justice and his treatment under detention. On April 15th he continued his testimony upon the same subject for upwards of half an hour. The Inspector suddenly interrupted with the statement that he was going to "cut all this out of the record." After discussion with me, he sent for Chief Inspector Augustus P. Schell, to whom the Inspector and I explained the situation. Inspector Schell, after seeking to dissuade me from pressing the claim of criminal creation of evidence against agents of the Department of Justice—"a department of the Government"—instructed the Inspector not to permit me to proceed unless the agents of the Department of Justice were present; to adjourn the hearing if necessary, and to cancel Cannone's bail "if he thought he would not appear."

The Inspector construed these instructions as requiring *me* to procure by subpœna (under the Rules, obtainable only by my filing a written statement of intention to prove material facts by the persons for whom subpœna is asked) the attendance of the agents of the Department of Justice. I explained that I would not offer agents of the Department of Justice as credible witnesses, and that my purpose in requesting the attendance of Agent Scully had not been to call him as a witness on behalf of Cannone, but to give Cannone opportunity to say whether or not Agent Scully was one of the persons guilty of criminal practices. I then offered to proceed to prove my case by the testimony of Cannone.

"Well, you've got to furnish *proof*," said the Inspector. "You can't prove anything by this man" (indicating Cannone). "This man is not a witness. HE IS THE ALIEN."

He ruled that no further testimony could be received as to the conduct of the agents of the Department of Justice, and struck out most of the testimony which Cannone had given—not in the ordinary juridical sense of "striking out"; Cannone's testimony was literally and bodily eliminated. * * *

(Signed)   WALTER NELLES,
                              138 *West 13th Street, New York.*

Subscribed and sworn to before me this 28th day of April, 1920.

                              ALBERT D. SILVER,
                                   Notary Public, Kings Co.

Cert. filed N. Y. Co. #359.

EXHIBIT 10.

EXTRACTS FROM CONFIDENTIAL INSTRUCTIONS
AUGUST 12, 1919.

Department of Justice,
Bureau of Investigation,
Washington, Aug. 12, 1919.

To all Special Agents and Employees:

The bureau requires a vigorous and comprehensive investigation of anarchistic and similar classes, Bolshevism, and kindred agitations advocating change in the present form of government by force or violence, the promotion of sedition and revolution, bomb throwing, and similar activities. In the present state of the Federal law this investigation should be particularly directed to persons not citizens of the United States, with a view of obtaining deportation cases. * * *

(4) In the investigation of all cases agents will report the evidence in form required by this bureau. *In making daily or partial reports all information of every nature, whether hearsay or otherwise, shall be included.* Inasmuch as gossip or said hearsay evidence is of no value in making technical proof, agents are hereby instructed to trace every piece of information to its source. * * *

(16) *Special agents will constantly keep in mind the necessity of preserving the cover of our confidential informants, and in no case shall they rely upon the testimony of such cover informants during deportation proceedings.*

W. J. FLYNN,
Director, Bureau of Investigation.

EXHIBIT 11.

CONFIDENTIAL INSTRUCTIONS, DEC. 27, 1919.

"DEPARTMENT OF JUSTICE.

Bureau of Investigation.

Washington, December 27, 1919.

Strictly Confidential.

Geo. E. Kelleher, Esq.,
Box 3185, Boston, Mass.

DEAR SIR:

I have already transmitted to you two briefs prepared in this department upon the COMMUNIST PARTY OF AMERICA and the COMMUNIST LABOR PARTY with instructions that these briefs be carefully examined and studied for the purpose of familiarizing yourself and the agents under your direction with the principles and tactics of these two respective organizations.

You have submitted to me affidavits upon various individuals connected with these respective organizations, stating that these persons are aliens and member of the organizations referred to. I have transmitted to the Commissioner General of Immigration the affidavits submitted by you with the request that warrants of arrest be issued at once. This action is now being taken by the Bureau of Immigration and warrants of arrest are being prepared and will shortly be forwarded to the immigration inspector of your district.

Briefly the arrangements which have been made are that the warrants will be forwarded to the immigration inspector who will at once communicate with you and advise you of the names of the persons for whom he has received warrants. You should then place under surveillance, where practicable, the persons mentioned and at the appointed time you will be advised by me by wire when to take into custody all persons for whom warrants have been issued.

At the time of the apprehension of these persons every effort should be made by you to definitely establish the fact that the persons arrested are members of either the COMMUNIST PARTY of America or the COMMUNIST LABOR PARTY. I have been reliably informed that instructions have been issued from the headquarters of each of these organizations to their members that they are to refuse to answer any questions put to them by any Federal officers and are to destroy all evidence of membership or affiliation with their respective organizations. It is, therefore, of the utmost importance that you at once make every effort to ascertain the location of all of the books and records of these organizations in your territory *and that the same be secured at the time of the arrests. As soon as the subjects are apprehended, you should endeavor to obtain from them, if possible, admissions that they are members of either of these parties, together with any statement concerning their citizenship status.* I cannot impress upon you too strongly the necessity of obtaining documentary evidence proving membership.

Particular efforts should be made to apprehend all of the officers of either of these two parties if they are aliens; *the residences of such officers should be searched in every instance for literature, membership cards, records and correspondence.* The meeting rooms should be thoroughly searched and an effort made to locate the charter of the COMMUNIST PARTY of America or the COMMUNIST LABOR PARTY, under which the local organization operates, as well as the membership and financial records which if not found in the meeting rooms of the organization will probably be found in the house of the recording and financial secretaries, respectively. *All literature, books, papers and anything hanging on the walls should be gathered up;* the ceilings and partitions should be sounded for hiding places. After obtaining any documentary evidence, the same should be wrapped up in packages and marked thereon, the location of the place, and the name of the persons obtaining the evidence and the contents of each package.

Violence towards any aliens should be scrupulously avoided. *Immediately upon apprehending an alien, he should be thoroughly searched.* *If found in groups in meeting rooms, they should be lined up against the wall and there searched;* particular attention being given to finding the membership book, in which connection the search of the pockets will not be sufficient. In no instance should money or other valuables be taken from the aliens. All documentary evidence taken from an alien should be placed in an individual envelope, provided for the purpose, which envelope should be marked showing the contents contained in the same, whether they were found in the possession of the alien or in his room, and if in the latter the address of the house should be given as well as the name of the alien and the officer who obtained the evidence. A duplicate record should be kept of all evidence thus obtained. At the time of the transfer of the alien to the immigration inspector, you should also turn over to the immigration inspector the original evidence obtained in the particular case, plainly marked so that there may be no complaint by the immigration officers as to the manner in which evidence has been collected by the agents of this Bureau.

I have made mention above that the meeting places and residences of the members should be thoroughly searched. *I leave it entirely to your discretion as to the method by which you should gain access to such places.* *If, due to the local conditions in your territory, you find that it is absolutely necessary for you to obtain a search warrant for the premises, you should communicate with the local authorities a few hours before the time for the arrests is set and request a warrant to search the premises.*

Under no conditions are you to take into your confidence the local police authorities or the state authorities prior to the making of the arrests. It is not the intention nor the desire of this office that American citizens, members of the two organizations be arrested at this time. *If, however, they are taken into custody any American citizens, through error and who are members of the COMMUNIST PARTY OF AMERICA or the COMMUNIST LABOR PARTY, you should immediately refer their cases to the local authorities.*

It may be necessary, in order to successfully make the arrests that you obtain the assistance of the local authorities at the time of the arrests. This action should not be taken, unless it is absolutely necessary; but I well appreciate that where a large number of arrests are to be made it may be impossible for the same to be made by special agents of this Department, in which event you are authorized to request the assistance of the local police authorities. *Such assistance should not be requested until a few hours before the time set for the arrests, in order that no "leak" may occur. It is to be distinctly understood that the arrests made are being made under the direction and supervision of the Department of Justice.*

For your own personal information, I have to advise you that the tentative date fixed for the arrests of the COMMUNISTS is Friday evening, January 2, 1920. This date may be changed, due to the fact that all of the immigration warrants may not be issued by that time. You will, however, be advised by telegraph as to the exact date and hour when the arrests are to be made.

If possible you should arrange with your under-cover informants to have meetings of the COMMUNIST PARTY and the COMMUNIST LABOR PARTY held on the night set. I have been in-

formed by some of the bureau officers that such arrangements will be made. This, of course, would facilitate the making of the arrests.

On the evening of the arrests, this office will be open the entire night and I desire that you *communicate by long distance to Mr. Hoover** any matters of vital importance or interest which may arise during the course of the arrests. *You will possibly be given from seven o'clock in the evening until seven o'clock in the morning to conclude the arrests and examinations.* As pointed out previously, the grounds for deportation in these cases will be based solely upon membership in the COMMUNIST PARTY of America or the COMMUNIST LABOR PARTY and for that reason it will not be necessary for you to go in detail into the particular activities of the persons apprehended. It is, however, desirable that wherever possible you should obtain additional evidence upon the individuals, particularly those who are leaders and officers in the local organizations. The immigration inspector will be under instructions to cooperate with you fully and I likewise desire that you cooperate in the same manner with the Immigration Inspector at the time of the arrests, as well as following the arrests. At the hearings before the Immigration Inspector you should render any and all reasonable assistance to the immigration authorities, both in the way of offering your services to them and the services of any of your stenographic force. It is of the utmost necessity that these cases be expedited and disposed of at the earliest possible moment and for that reason stenographic assistance and any assistance necessary should be rendered by you to the immigration inspectors. *An excellent spirit of cooperation exists between the Commissioner-General of Immigration** and this Department in Washington* and I desire that the same spirit of cooperation between the field officers of this Bureau and the field officers of the Bureau of Immigration also exist.

I desire that the morning following the arrests you should forward to this office by special delivery marked for the *"Attention of Mr. Hoover"** a complete list of the names of the persons arrested, with an indication of residence, or organization to which they belong, and whether or not they were included in the original list of warrants. *In cases where arrests are made of persons not covered by warrants,* you should at once request the local immigration authorities for warrants in all such cases and you should also communicate with this office at the same time. I desire also that the morning following the arrests that you communicate in detail by telegram, *"Attention of Mr. Hoover,"** the results of the arrests made, giving the total number of persons of each organization taken into custody, together with a statement of any interesting evidence secured.

The above cover the general instructions to be followed in these arrests and the same will be supplemented by telegraphic instructions at the proper time.

Very truly yours,   FRANK BURKE,
                                    Assistant Director and Chief.

NOTE by the Editor: In the foregoing instructions it will be observed: (1) That the Department of Justice assumed on Dec. 27, 1919, that both the Com-

---

*J. E. Hoover, Special Assistant to the Attorney General.
**Mr. Caminetti.

munist Party and the Communist Labor Party were unlawful organizations, whereas the Secretary of Labor, upon whom alone the duty fell of deciding the question, did not decide until a month later that the Communist Party was unlawful (Jan. 24, 1920), and decided four months later that the Communist Labor Party was perfectly lawful (May 5, 1920). (2) That warrants may be dispensed with at discretion of local agents. (3) That "under cover informants" are to bring about meetings on Jan. 2 to facilitate wholesale arrests.

EXHIBIT 12.

CONFIDENTIAL INSTRUCTIONS (two sets) which were issued individually to the Dept. of Justice agents in New England who were to conduct the raids of Jan. 2, 1920.

"INSTRUCTIONS TO AGENTS.

1. Each person named in the warrant to be taken into custody.

2. Upon taking person into custody *try to obtain all documentary evidence possible* to establish membership in the COMMUNIST PARTY, including membership cards, books, correspondence etc.

3. Also *try to secure charters, meeting minutes, membership books, due books, membership correspondence, etc., in possession of such person*, which may lead to further investigations of members not yet known.

4. All such evidence secured, as above, to be properly marked and sealed as belonging to such person, with name of arrestee, place where secured, date secured, and by whom secured marked plainly on same.

5. *Person or persons taken into custody not to be permitted to communicate with any outside person until after examination by this office and until permission is given by this office.*

6. Upon making arrest, *person in custody to be brought to the place designated by this office for a preliminary examination.*

7. *Preliminary examination to be made by Agent making arrest on forms provided for that purpose by this office.* This form to be followed closely and filled out in detail. The form then to be read to person in custody for him to sign and swear to same. If he refuses to swear and sign to same, then Agent, in presence of one witness to examination, to sign and swear to same and to have witness do the same.

8. *If a person claims American citizenship, he must produce documentary evidence of same.* If native born, through birth records. If naturalized, through producing for Agent copy of naturalization papers. Be sure that these papers are final papers, containing words "and is hereby admitted to become a citizen of the United States."

9. In case of any uncertainty as to citizenship or non-citizenship of person taken into custody, or for any other reason, consult the office.

10. Absolutely no publicity or information to be given by an agent. All such requests for information to be referred to Division Superintendent. Also request observances above by assisting officers."

———

"1. At the time of apprehension, every effort must be made to establish definitely the fact that one arrested is a member of either the Communist Party of America or Communist Labor Party.

2. It is of utmost importance to make every effort to ascertain location of all books and records of these organizations, and that same be secured at time of arrest.

3. Upon making arrests, *endeavor to secure admissions* as to membership, in Communist and Communist Labor Parties, together with any possible documentary proof.

4. *Endeavor apprehend officers of either party of aliens, searching residences for literature, membership cards, records and correspondence.*

5. Search meeting rooms and endeavor to locate charters of Communist or Communist Labor Parties, as well as membership and financial records, which, however, may be found at homes of Recording and Financial Secretaries. *Literature, books, papers and anything on the walls should be gathered up,* and ceilings and partitions sounded for hiding places. Wrap anything taken and mark the location of place, names of persons obtaining evidence, and contents of each.

6. *Upon apprehension, aliens should be searched thoroughly; if found in groups in meeting rooms, line them up against the wall and there search them.* Take anything which tends to establish connection with either Communist or Communist Labor Parties, in other words, only such materials referring to these parties, and nothing distinctly personal such as money and other valuables. Mark envelopes showing contents; whether found in possession of alien or in his room, with address, as well as names of those obtaining evidence. Duplicate record of all this should be kept; original evidence obtained in the cases to be turned over to the Immigration Officers.

7. *Only aliens should be arrested; if American citizens are taken by mistake, their cases should be immediately referred to the local authorities.*

8. Arrest of members covered by warrants to be made Friday, at 9 P. M. Only aliens, and connected with Communist and Communist Labor Parties; make preliminary examination as per office memorandum.

NOTE: These instructions are extremely confidential; are issued only for the guidance of authorized agents of this office; are charged to such agents and must be returned to this office upon completion of assignment."

EXHIBIT 13.

THE "COLYER CASE."

MORRIS KATZEFF, Petitioner,

vs.

HENRY J. SKEFFINGTON, Comm'r of Immigration.

Before District Court of the United States, Anderson, J.

Boston, April, 1920.

This case came before Judge Anderson on three petitions for *habeas corpus* involving eighteen relators, arrested on or about January 3, 1920, as aliens subject to deportation because of their membership in the Communist Party.

The evidence showed generally the following:

During the night of Friday, January 2-3, 1920, in New England, there were arrested by the Department of Justice, Mr. and Mrs. William T. Colyer, British subjects, together with several hundred other aliens and citizens. Warrants of arrest, wherever inconvenient to obtain, were dispensed with by the express direction of Washington; in the large majority of cases no warrants were in existence and no cause for their issuance had been shown. Meetings of Communists, to be held on the particular night of January 2, had been stimulated by Department of Justice undercover agents, so as to facilitate arrests. Men and women were taken up wholesale, at meetings, on the streets, or at their homes. Equally without search-warrants, the offices and homes of the prisoners were entered and ransacked, and writings, books and other property carried away These several hundred citizens and aliens were then handcuffed, bundled into motor-cars, and taken to police stations, jails or any convenient place of detention, there to await the slow process of inquisition (without counsel), and classification. Food, water and bedding were usually not provided. The citizens were gradually weeded out, and told to go home. Some aliens also were liberated; the rest were taken to Boston, in some cases handcuffed and chained and marched through the streets for newspaper photographers to snap them, and were finally imprisoned on Deer Island, without sanitary conveniences, without blankets or mattresses, and exposed to cold from broken windows. After the arrests and imprisonment, warrants of arrest were asked, and obtained, from the Department of Labor in Washington. Bail was fixed in such amount, up to $10,000, as would reasonably insure the impossibility of raising it. Other conditions were such as reasonably to insure that the prisoners should not too soon communicate with friends or lawyers.

Three months later, Morris Katzeff, of the Boston Bar, proceeded with the help of counsel to lay these facts before Judge Anderson, on a petition for writs of *habeas corpus* for Mr. and Mrs. Colyer and sixteen other aliens, alleging violation of Constitutional rights, particularly that of "due process of law." A long trial was had. Judge Anderson, overruling objections by government counsel, insisted on looking into the facts, even to the extent of compelling Department employees to explain just how they had acted, and by whose instructions. During the course of the trial, as the facts gradually came out, Judge Anderson delivered various remarks from the bench, such as the following:

"This case seems to have been conducted under that modern theory of statesmanship that you hang first and try afterwards. * * *

"A more lawless proceeding it is hard for anybody to conceive. Talk about Americanization! What we need is to Americanize people that are carrying on such proceedings as this. We shall forget everything we ever learned about American Constitutional Liberty if we are to undertake to justify such a proceeding as this. * * *

"It is the business of any American citizen, who knows anything about Americanism, to resign if given such instructions. * * *

"What does appear, beyond reasonable dispute, is that the Government owns and operates some part of the Communist Party."

Particular aspects of the case will be set forth under appropriate heads.

I.

ACTIVITY OF THE DEPARTMENT OF JUSTICE.

The Boston Commissioner of Immigration, Mr. Skeffington, being on the stand, the Court questioned him as follows with regard to the activity of the Department of Justice in connection with the raids of January 1920 (typewritten record, pages 70 *et seq.*) :

Q. After the armistice your Department had, as I understand it, entire legal control over deportations; is that so as you understand it?
A. Yes, sir; no other department of the Government has the power to deport.
Q. *Is there any statute to your knowledge giving the Department of Justice any power with relation to deportation?*
A. *No, sir.*

Further questioning by the Court brought out the proper course of procedure, as follows (testimony of Skeffington, page 72) :

"The method was for the Department of Justice agents to send their evidence in the form of an affidavit to the Department of Justice at Washington. They brought it over to the Department of Labor and asked that a warrant on that information be issued. * * * Later they were ordered to show us the evidence that they had before they sent it to Washington, and if we agreed on it then we notified our Department that we agreed that a warrant should be issued in the case of John Doe."

Having thus ascertained the extent to which the Department of Justice could lawfully proceed in the premises, in cooperation with the Immigration authorities, the Court by subsequently questioning another witness discovered how much further the activities of the Department of Justice were actually carried (testimony of James A. Sullivan, Deputy Immigration Commissioner at Boston, pages 162 *et seq.*) :

(By Mr. Katzeff :)

Q. Did Agents of the Department of Justice exercise the power, or a power, to release men who were detained at Deer Island?
A. Unless we had a warrant for them. * * *
The Court: *Did you have people there without warrants that Department of Justice Agents released?*
The Witness: *The Department of Justice had a number of people there without warrants.* If they released them * * * I have no record of it.
Q. You mean——

The Court: Just a minute. I want to get that. When you went down there, or during this proceeding, *do I understand you to state that there were people there in the barracks that you had charge of, brought there by the Department of Justice, for whom you had no warrant and who were discharged by the Department of Justice because you had no warrant?*
The Witness: *Yes, sir.*

It was further brought out, from Sullivan, that the Department of Justice from the time of the raid had a man on Deer Island, who later *assumed control over the payment and hiring of the guards on the Island.* Stenographic assistance and interpreters were also supplied to the immigration authorities by the Department of Justice.

The Department of Justice Agents also took part in the hearings of aliens after they had been turned over to the immigration authorities. Mr. Sullivan testified that prior to January 27th or 28th, *the customary procedure was to examine the alien after he had been delivered to Deer Island, without giving him an opportunity to be represented at that time by counsel.* This was called the "preliminary hearing," *before undergoing which the alien would not be admitted to bail.* The subsequent hearings, that is, the continuation of the hearing held after the Government had obtained what evidence it wanted, is called in the record a "rehearing." At the so-called rehearing, aliens were allowed counsel for the first time. The Department of Justice representative was present both at the so-called hearing and rehearing.

On the question of the *amount of bail* in which the aliens were held, it appeared, too, that the agents of the Department of Justice were active, making their recommendation to the inspectors.

Witness John A. Ryder, Immigration Inspector, Boston District, testified that he had had a number of years experience trying cases of anarchists, immoralists, criminals, prostitutes, and the general run of aliens, but that *never before the present time* had any Department of Justice official or any one else acting in analogy to a prosecuting officer, been present and participated in deportation hearings.

Witness Sullivan testified that *censoring of prisoners' letters* at Deer Island was delegated to the Department of Justice.

The witness Valkenburgh (Record p. 1117) testified that he was an agent of the Department of Justice, and participated with three other Department agents and three police officers in the raid on 885 Washington St; that 29 persons were arrested in that raid; that they were searched, and that exhibits were taken by the raiding party from the hall. Though witness had 16 Labor Department warrants in his possession, *none of them were used in the arrest of these 29 persons; and the raiding party had no search warrants.* All the arrestees were locked up over night; the next morning seven who were citizens were released; the other 22 were forwarded to Deer Island. Questioning by the Court:

Q. And you took 7 citizens and put them in cells and kept them over night, as you say now?
A. I found out later that they were citizens.
Q. Is that your notion of liberty under the law?
A. I had no other way of finding out they were citizens. They didn't tell me as such until the next morning.

Mr. Goldberg (Government counsel) : I suggest, if your Honor please, that it was this agent's business to obey his instructions, or resign.

The Court. *Well, that may be true, but it is the business of any American citizen, who knows anything about Americanism, to resign if given such instructions. That is all.*

A typical witness was Ivan T. Hrynchuk (page 1088 of the Record). He was arrested the night of January 2nd, and was confined at Deer Island continuously until released by habeas corpus in April. His person was searched at time of arrest, and exhibits thus obtained were used at his hearing. No warrant of arrest or search warrant had existed.

Witness testified his hearing at Deer Island was completed before he was notified of the right to be assisted by counsel. *The court pointed out that though witness was arrested January 2nd, his warrant was dated January 17th, and declared—*

"This case seems to have been conducted under that modern theory of statesmanship that you hang first and try afterwards."

Counsel for the government, objecting to this remark, contended that such procedure had support in court decisions, The following then occurred:

The Court: Can you cite any case which supports the proposition that the Department of Justice can go out without any piece of paper or warrant, or, so far as appears, any investigation, and seize men, put them in jail and hold them there two weeks, and then get warrants and put them through a trial of this kind and call that due process of law?

Mr. Goldberg: I don't know what your Honor means by a "trial of this kind;" but if your Honor refers to having a preliminary hearing in the absence of counsel, and then permitting counsel to come in afterwards, yes, I can cite a number of cases in the Supreme Court of the United States upholding that as due process.

The Court: I think I am fairly familiar with those cases. *I know of nothing which lays the slightest foundation for any such proceeding as this.* A more lawless proceeding it is hard for anybody to conceive. Talk about Americanization! What we need is to Americanize people that are carrying on such proceedings as this. *We shall forget everything we ever learned about American Constitutional liberty if we are to undertake to justify such a proceeding as this.*

Mr. Goldberg: I am not responsible for the departmental policies.

The Court: I know you are not, but I can hardly sit here on this bench as an American citizen and restrain my indignation at such proceedings.

II. UNLAWFUL ARRESTS, SEARCHES AND SEIZURES.

The Court questioned the Commissioner of Immigration, Mr. Skeffington, as to the procedure followed in the raids of January 2nd and 3rd (Pages 79 et seq.):

(By the Court:)

Q. Just a moment on that, Mr. Skeffington. Were these arrests for what you call the "raids" made by your forces, or by the Department of Justice?

A. Department of Justice, your Honor.

Q. Did your people have anything to do with them?

A. Yes.

Q. What?

A. We ordered our men to take the warrants, say for Manchester, New Hampshire, go to a police station and sit there, and when these men were brought in connect them up with the warrants.

Q. What do you mean by "connect them up with the warrants"?

*A. That is, see whether or not we had a warrant for them, and if we had we took them. * * * They didn't carry the warrants with them.* They brought the persons to the Police Station and there the warrants were awaiting them.

Q. Can you point out any rule or any statute under which the Department of Justice agents have power to arrest?

A. No, I don't know anything about that, Judge, except that we were working under rule. We didn't have the men. They had to furnish them, and they did furnish them.

Q. Did you have instructions as to this procedure?

A. We had an understanding.

Q. Written instructions?

A. No. We had a conference in Washington in the Department of Labor with Mr. Hoover and another gentleman of the Department of Justice.

Q. Who is Mr. Hoover?

A. Mr. Hoover is an officer in the Department of Justice.

Mr. Goldberg: *Special Assistant to the Attorney General.*

Deputy Commissioner Sullivan also testified that approximately one hundred warrants were requested by telegraph after the main raid on the evening of January 2nd. His examination on this point follows:

Q. But there were more than 100 warrants?

A. I should say so.

(By the Court:)

Q. Were any of those in custody before the telegraphic warrants were applied for?

The Witness: Yes, sir.

The Court: About how many?

The Witness: About 100, I should judge, it might be more.

Q. *You mean 100 men were in custody at Deer Island before the telegraphic warrants were applied for?*

(Objection; overruled; question repeated to witness.)

A. *A hundred men or more were detained at Deer Island without warrants, yes, sir.*

The evidence of Messrs. Skeffington and Sullivan was corroborated by George E. Kelleher, Division Superintendent of the Bureau of Investigation of the Department of Justice, headquarters in Boston, Mass., who had charge of rounding up the aliens in Massachusetts, New Hampshire and Vermont. His testimony on the point of illegal arrests was as follows:

Q. What authority, what written document, did you have in your possession for the arrest of the individuals that were arrested that night?

(Objection; overruled.)

A. The authority that we had, the instructions from tne Department at Washington, and the knowledge that warrants were waiting for many of those who were picked up, *that those who were members of the Communist party could be picked up and detained while warrants were being telegraphed and asked for.*
Q. It is a fact, is it not, Mr. Kelleher, that men and women were picked up that night without any warrant in your possession for their custody?

(Objection; overruled.)

A. That is so.

Counsel for the relators then went on to examine the witness (p. 235) with regard to his procedure pursuant to the secret instructions of Dec. 27th issued for the raid from Washington (Exh. 11 herewith).

Q. Did your men search the bodies and the homes and the halls at which the various men and women were arrested?

(Exception; overruled.)

A. Yes.
Q. And they made seizure, did they not, of papers, documents, books and what not?

(Objection; overruled.)

A. Pursuant to the Department's instruction. * * * *The instructions that were read into the record this morning were paraphrased, and each agent was given a copy of those same instructions only in brief form for his guidance.* (The witness is referring to the instructions Exh. 12 herewith.)
* * *
The examination then proceeded:

Q. Therefore, one is justified in asking, Mr. Kelleher, whether or not it is a fact that searches were made by the arresting officers irrespective of the production of a search warrant for the search?

(Objection; overruled.)

A. *As you will note in the original instructions, that was left to the discretion of the various officers.* In other words, it appeared to those in charge of those particular things that where a person would probably permit us to search anyhow, it would be a *needless waste of time, when under such tremendous pressure, to apply for the search warrant,* that the person would permit us to search the place without it.

Counsel then returned once more (page 248) to the question of unlawful arrests and detentions:

Q. What did you do with those whom the warrant did not fit, or who did not fit the warrant?

(Objection; overruled.)

A. *They were detained.* * * *
The Court: Detained where?
The Witness: They were detained at the station or brought to Boston and taken down to Deer Island. * * *
Q. What was the authority upon which you were acting when you took men and women for whom there were no outstanding warrants?

(Objection; overruled.)

A. The Department's instructions.
Q. You arrested people, you then checked up those whom you arrested with the list of warrants in the hands of the Immigration officials, and where there was a lack of warrant you continued to hold onto your arrestee?

(Objection; overruled.)

A. *If he fitted the description as a member of either the Communist Party or the Communist Labor Party and was an alien.*

At the instance of the Court, counsel then went on to ask the witness "just how these people that went around to the halls and homes were instructed, if they were given lists of names or given descriptions of places and persons, or how they knew what places they were to raid and whom they were to bring to the concentration points." The witness replied that they tried as far as possible to get the aliens in groups, at meetings, for example; "our agents went where meetings were being held to our knowledge and sorted them out according to either whether we had warrants for them *or whether they were alien members of the Communist or Communist Labor Parties.*"

The next witness was William J. West, Assistant Division Superintendent, Bureau of Investigation, Department of Justice. He testified (page 272):

A. *In some instances* the Immigration officers no doubt had the warrants, and the aliens were brought in to them, the agent having in his possession also a list of persons named in the warrants. That accounts for those who were arrested on the warrants. *As I have already stated, that night there were meetings of the Communist party held in various cities and towns about Massachusetts and New Hampshire, and those meeting places were visited and the persons found therein were questioned individually as to whether or not they were members of the Communist party or of the Communist Labor party, and as to whether or not they were aliens or citizens.* That is where the sorting out process occurred. Those persons who admitted being members of the Communist party, or of the Communist Labor Party, and who admitted being aliens, *were immediately set aside and questioned further.*
Q. Who questioned them, Mr. West? Who questioned them? Officials of your staff?
A. Agents from my office.
Q. Agents? Did they apprise them of what their legal rights and constitutional rights were, as to the right to withhold any information unless there was a lawful warrant for their arrest?

(Objection; overruled.)

A. I don't know what occurred in each particular case.
Q. Did you instruct them to tell the people before they spoke that they had a right to consult counsel and that what they said would be used against them?
A. No, sir.
Q. In fact, the instruction was to get information from them as much as possible?
A. *The instructions were to secure such evidence as would connect them with membership in the Communist party or Communist Labor party.*

The witness then testified that persons were taken into custody for whom no warrants had been issued, if such persons confessed to being aliens and members of either of the proscribed parties; that they were then put through the regular questionnaire, and warrants requested for them by telephone and telegraph. Statistically, the witness testified to the following figures (page 274):

Q. The facts that we are after, Mr. West, ought to take just three minutes to obtain—namely, how many men and women were taken into custody? Approximately how many were there? Do you know?
A. No, sir, I do not.
Q. Were there 2,000 or 1,000?
A. I should estimate it at approximately 600 persons.
Q. 600? Then finally there were at Deer Island only, as you told us, about 440?
A. Yes, sir.
Q. So that you let go about 160?
A. Approximately that.
Q. And of those that you took into custody—namely, 440, or whatever it was that you took into custody—there were no warrants for approximating about 100?

(Objection; overruled.)

A. That is approximately true; yes, sir.

Later in the examination of the same witness (Mr. West), counsel for the relators turned again to the question of unlawful search and seizure. Quoting from the secret instructions of December 27, counsel called the attention of the witness to the following: "Particular efforts should be made to apprehend all of the officers of either of these two parties if they are aliens. The residences of such officers should be searched in every instance for literature, membership cards, records and correspondence." Witness was asked whether he had given oral instructions to his agents "relative to getting into residences and what they should do if they got in?" Witness replied that that was left to the discretion of the individual agent, who was to conduct himself as local conditions required. Witness also stated that in certain cases search warrants had, to his information, been obtained. Then comes the following (page 305):

(By Mr. Brooks:)

Q. Do you know what was seized under these search warrants in Worcester and Lawrence?

(Objection; overruled.)

A. Not in detail.
Q. Well, generally speaking?
A. Generally speaking, evidence tending to show that the persons taken into custody were connected with one or the other of the proscribed parties.
Q. That is to say, papers, books, pictures, and so forth?
A. No, I don't know about pictures. There were some books. But papers principally.

(By the Court:)

Q. Well, you knew, Mr. West, that no search warrants could be obtained under the laws of the United States or of the Commonwealth of Massachusetts which would authorize the seizure of such literature or evidence as you were after, didn't you? Otherwise stated, this was not outlaw property within the laws of the United States or the Commonwealth, was it?

(Objection; overruled.)

A. Well, I submit I do not know, your Honor. I would have to submit that question to the office of the United States Attorney, as to what would be outlaw property and what would be seizable under either the United States warrants or the State warrants.

Q. Well, if you instructed your agent to get a warrant to seize concealed weapons, for instance—I think there is a statute covering that—*but the real purpose of the warrant was not to seize weapons but to seize literature,* and it was intended to be used for another purpose than that which on its face it appeared to be obtained for, wasn't that——

(Objection; overruled.)

A. If those warrants were issued as gun warrants——
Q. As what?
A. *As gun warrants—that is, as warrants to seize guns, weapons—and anything else other than guns and weapons were seized, why, it would naturally follow that the property seized was not the property named in the search warrant.*

(By Mr. Brooks:)

Q. Did you caution your agents to confine themselves strictly to the subject matter of the warrant?

(Objection; overruled.)

A. I issued no instructions.
Q. You merely told them to secure search warrants where practicable—as I understand your phrase—"where practicable"?
A. Yes, sir.
Q. What did you instruct them to do where that was not practicable?
A. Where that was not practicable they were to follow the instructions contained in the Bureau letter of instructions.

Commenting on the methods brought out by the above testimony, the court remarked (page 308):

The Court: It is interesting to note that we are all finding out gradually what is meant by the 18th Amendment.
Mr. Kelleher: Are you referring to the 18th Amendment? If you are, your Honor, I would say that that does not come under the Bureau of Investigation, Department of Justice.
The Court: Doesn't it?
Mr. Brooks: Internal Revenue.
The Court: *The statutes which have been put in here so far indicate that the aliens do not come under the Department of Justice, but evidently they did on the 2nd of January.*

Further details as to the manner of arresting the aliens during the January 2nd raid were brought out by the examination of John A. Ryder, an Immigration Inspector in the Boston district. He testified as follows (page 444):

Q. Did you participate in any of the raids on the 2nd of January?
A. I was assigned to Brockton.
Q. Did you go to Brockton?
A. Yes, sir.
Q. How many warrants did you serve in Brockton?
A. I don't remember serving any. I had warrants. *I don't remember of identifying anybody with those warrants.*
Q. How many warrants did you have?
A. *Roughly, about 10.*
Q. And where were you with the warrants in Brockton?
A. I was in the City Marshal's office.
Q. And did the Department of Justice agent bring people before you?

(Objection; overruled.)

Q. About how many people did they bring before you for identification?
A. Oh, they were being brought in all night by the police.
Q. How many people,—about how many?

A. *Oh, at least a hundred.*

Q. At least a hundred,—men and women?

A. I would qualify that 100. I don't think there were a hundred—less than a hundred. *Between 50 and 100.*

Q. *Nearer a hundred than fifty?*

A. *I think so.* That night and the next day.

Q. And there was not one out of the fifty or seventy-five, or close to a hundred, that fit any of the names on the warrants?

A. Yes; afterwards it was found that they did.

Q. *But that night you did not serve a single warrant?*

A. *No.*

Q. Were they all released?

A. *No; 18 or 19 were brought to Boston the next day.* * * *

Q. When you brought them to Boston there were no warrants for their arrest?

A. Excepting in a few cases, yes.

Q. But about 18, you say, you wired on for telegraphic warrants for?

A. Yes.

Q. And were they examined by the Department of Justice agent on the questionnaire?

A. Yes, sir.

Q. And those who answered that they were members of the Communist party—were those the ones for whose arrest you applied for warrants?

A. Well, I did not take any direct part in that examination. I knew they were examining the aliens. Once in a while I would stroll over and I might butt in and say something. I did not think I had any connection with that. * * *

(By the Court:)

Q. Where did they pick up these people around Brockton? In the halls or in their homes?

A. In their homes. I might explain that very simply. The Financial Secretary having been brought in with his books of membership cards of the Communist Party of America, there was found to be about 200 on his register. So that they went looking up some of those people. And the Communist card was apparently good evidence against them to apply for a warrant at least.

Q. Well, you said they were doing it all night and a part of the next day.

A. Yes, sir; the police.

Q. Did they take these people out of bed and bring them to the police station during the night?

A. Why, there was a group of police officials assigned to assist the Department of Justice, and they knew the territory and they were sent out.

Q. Well, that went on in the evening and all through the late hours of the morning?

A. Yes, your Honor.

Q. You stayed there at the station to see if you could fit any of these people to the warrants you had?

A. Yes, sir.

Q. *And you did not find a single fit in your case?*

A. *No.* I was upstairs and they were brought in and detained down stairs, and a great many would be brought in without my knowledge.

Q. What did they do with them? Lock them up?

A. After a few moments, then each one would be brought upstairs and questioned and let go in many cases.

Q. In other cases what did they do?

A. Held them there.

Q. Locked them up?

A. Yes, your Honor.

III.

DELEGATION OF WORK BY DEPARTMENT OF JUSTICE TO PRIVATE INDIVIDUALS AND LOCAL POLICE.

It was brought out, during the examination of George E. Kelleher, Division Superintendent of the Bureau of Investigation of the Department of Justice, headquarters in Boston, that to some extent the Department, in conducting the January 2nd raids, availed itself of the assistance of volunteer private individuals. The witness was testifying as to the number of persons who participated in the raids within his jurisdiction, and had set that number at from 300 to 500. He was then examined as to the nature of the force (page 228):

Q. Whom have you in mind, what section of officials or individuals have you in mind when you give the number as from 300 to 500?
A. The agents of the Department of Justice, and the police authorities of the various cities where the raids were carried out.
Q. Nobody else except agents for the Department of Justice and the police authorities?
A. No.
Q. Any volunteer private citizens?
A. Volunteer private citizens who donated their automobiles. Our force was increased to some extent through the re-employment of men who had previously been in our employ and who knew how to operate as agents.
* * *
Q. It is admitted by you, Mr. Kelleher, that in the party under your control making the arrests on the evening of January 2nd there were persons other than officials of the Department of Justice and officials of the various police forces in the various cities?
A. Only so far as the question of transportation is concerned. The men who participated in the arrests were either police officials or on the payroll of the Department of Justice.
Q. You mean, men who actually took hold of the bodies of the men and women who were arrested?
A. Yes.
Q. But assistance was rendered you in the raid by other than officials either of the Department of Justice or the police force of this Commonwealth?
A. In the matter of transportation. * * *
Q. You did not take a definite census of those who volunteered, did you?
A. It would be impossible. We might be able to get a man for one trip and then lose him because he had other business to attend to. I have qualified that, however, by stating that it was entirely a matter of transportation. We tried to make it as easy as possible for those who were taken in raids, particularly in the case of women. *Rather than to force them to walk long distances we tried to provide automobiles for their convenience.(!)*

IV.

PROVOCATIVE AGENTS.

The confidential letter of instructions of Dec. 27th, sent to the Division Superintendent of the Boston branch of the Bureau of Investigation, George E. Kelleher, by Frank Burke, Assistant Director and Chief of the Bureau of Investigation, Department of Justice, Washington, D. C., contains the following instruction (Ex. 11 herewith):

"If possible, you should arrange with your under-cover informants to have meetings of the **COMMUNIST PARTY** and the **COMMUNIST LABOR PARTY** held on the night set. I have been informed by some of the bureau offices that such arrangements will be made. This, of course, would facilitate the making of the arrests."

George E. Kelleher was examined upon this point, and gave the following testimony (page 250):

Q. You had good reason to know about some of these meetings, did you not?
A. Yes.
Q. You had even reason to know that the meeting would be held, did you not?
A. Yes.
Q. *And in some instances you even stimulated the calling of the meeting, did you not?*

(Objection; overruled.)

A. *Possibly.* It may be that that did not apply in this particular district; it may be that it did. I will have to refer you to Mr. West, who is in more direct touch with that entire situation.
Q. But it may be that it did?
A. Yes.
Q. *In other words, the meeting was arranged at which these people were to be found?*
A. *There is that possibility.*
Q. And that possibility is not excluded in the instructions which you got from Washington.
A. Not at all.
Q. In fact, that possibility is included in the instructions which you got from Washington?
A. Yes, sir.

In reply to a direct question by the court, whether the witness had ever given instructions personally to act under that instruction from Washington, witness replied that

"upon the receipt of those instructions they were handed to Mr. West, who took appropriate steps under those instructions. I never came in direct and personal contact with any of the so-called informers."

(By the Court:)

Q. *Have you any present knowledge of the extent to which the Communist Party and the Communist Labor Party are under cover in that way?*

(Objection.)

A. *It would be very hard for anyone in Boston, or anywhere outside of Washington, to make any answer to that question.*
Q. And I suppose you do not know when that Government participation in the Communist Party and the Communist Labor Party began do you?

Mr. Goldberg: If your Honor please, while I realize it is a matter of interest, is that a matter of consequence in these proceedings?
The Court: It is of the most vital consequence.

(Objection; overruled.)

Q. You do not know personally when it began, do you?
A. No, I have no knowledge.
Q. And I understand you to say you do not have personal knowledge of the extent of the participation in this district, that Mr. West would know rather than you?
A. Yes. I would have an idea as to how it might come up, because the employment of any man who might be paid by the Department of Justice appropriation, who might be connected with such an organization for Government purposes, would naturally have to come through my hands,—*appointed by Washington and sent to this district by the Washington authorities.*

Witness was then asked how many under-cover informants were operating in his district, and replied he did not know; that the number is constantly changing by the addition of new men or the removal of others from the district.

The Court asked the witness whether he didn't think the system of under-cover informants was exceedingly dangerous:—"Somebody who is employed to go around under an alias or pseudonym, or some kind of disguise, to pretend to be a Communist or Socialist or Anarchist, when in fact he is in the employ of an entirely different organization and is operating for entirely different purposes—that is an exceedingly dangerous thing, isn't it?" Witness replied that he did not think so, since the purpose of the cover informant working for the government was to be animated solely by the desire to do a service for the government. Witness admitted, however, that the system provided for the keeping of a watch by one informant on the other; and said further that he regarded it as a wise thing to have the informants keep a watch on each other.

WILLIAM J. WEST was then examined as to his knowledge of the activities of the under-cover informants, and though extremely evasive, finally confirmed Kelleher's testimony:

Q. You remember the instructions, Mr. West?
A. I remember the instructions; yes, sir.
Q. *Did you impart those instructions to your cover informants?*
A. *I cannot say.*
Q. *You are not prepared to deny it?*
A. *I am not.*
Q. *And presumably you acted upon instructions that came to you from your chief at Washington, did you not?*
A. *I in each instance carried out all instructions issued to me, to the best of my knowledge.*
Q. And do you recall there were specific instructions to hold meetings that night?
A. I recall; yes, sir.
The Court: Were Communist meetings actually held that night?
The Witness: Yes, sir.
The Court: In large numbers?
The Witness: On the night of January 2 there were Communist meetings held at Worcester, there was a meeting at the city headquarters in Boston, there was a meeting at Nashua, N. H., I believe there was a meeting in Lynn, I believe a meeting in Springfield.
Q. What was the earliest you knew the meetings would be held on that night?

(Objection; overruled.)

A. *To my knowledge, at the present time, the earliest that I can now recall of having advance notice of a meeting on the night of January 2 was several days prior to January 2.*

Later in the examination of the same witness, counsel for the relators reverted to the under-cover informants. He could elicit the information only that deportation work was a new departure for the Department of Justice, leaving the inference that the informants "were people especially trained, if not specially obtained, for this class of work, of a rather temporary character"; that there were informants who, to the knowledge of the witness, operated in the Boston and related districts on radical work; that the Department of Justice had employed such informants since 1917, which was the date of the witness's first joining the Department.

V.

GENERAL CONDITIONS OF RAIDS.

There follow brief abstracts of the evidence of a few out of many witnesses, taken upon oath in this case.

Mrs. Stanislas Vasiliewska: Mother of three children; went with her little girl of 13 to a meeting in Low's Hall, Chelsea. Plain-clothes man and police er ered and ordered "Hands up," searched everyone, took down the pictures fro 1 the wall and the "No Smoking" sign in Russian, handcuffed the men two and two, took the witness and her child to the police station, locked them in a cell with another woman who was pregnant. At midnight the little girl w s sent home alone. Witness remained in police station until 8 or 9 A. M.; was then taken with two handcuffed men by Department of Justice agent to dock to await afternoon boat; was locked into the dock toilet with cigar butts, filth, etc. Later Mrs. Colyer was locked in with her. Witness did not know until a long time afterwards what had happened to her three children.

Charles Michaelson: American citizen; arrested 120 Market St., Lynn, where 39 persons had met to organize a Jewish Cooperative Bakery. Arrested by eight or nine men; searched, records taken; citizens and aliens separated but all taken to police station. Kept there from 9:30 Friday night until 12 noon Saturday, denied food and denied water; kept in the corridor in spite of fact that there were open cells. Denied chance to call up his wife on the telephone. Saturday noon 38 of the 39 arrested were released and told to go home, of whom 13 or 14 had been American citizens.

Minnie Federman: American citizen; arrested 6 A. M. January 3rd in her bedroom by six or seven men. No warrant shown. Was refused permission to dress in the next room; dressed in the closet while officer held the handle of the door. Room searched, mattress ripped up; witness detained several hours at police station and city prison, and then released. Property taken from witness not returned.

Annie Valinskas: Married; mother of child of three. Arrested, Nassau, N. H. at St. John the Baptist Hall. All persons put under arrest, searched and men handcuffed. About 150 in all including about 13 women. Seven women released at police court and six held. Witness was shown suit case by federal officials which they said they had taken from her house. She denied ownership. They then showed her two prayer books which she identified as her own and her father's. Was shown neither warrant of arrest nor search warrant. Was confined with four other women in a cell 9 feet by 6, entirely unfurnished. Remained there from Friday night until Saturday afternoon.

Frank Mack: English subject, in this country 6 years; arrested at his house; demanded to be shown a warrant, was read a warrant which was unsigned and did not include his name. Taken to police station, put through third degree examination. Transported next day to Long Wharf where he saw a crowd of people in chains compelled by officers to pose for newspaper photographers. As to conditions on Deer Island, prisoners were provided with no sanitary conveniences and compelled to remain in unheated cells furnished only with a spring cot without blankets or mattress; the latter were later provided. Guards were very harsh and were under the authority of both the Department of Justice and Immigration officials. Sunday after arrival at Deer Island, witness requested permission for prisoners to gather for religious service, which was refused. At witness's hearing he was confronted with exhibits of radical literature which had been removed from his room, together with pocket book, keys, newspapers, cards, and several photographs and a book. This was the first information witness had had that his room had been searched.

Ernest Liberman: English subject; arrested without warrant at meeting; with other men was marched through the streets of Boston to Long Wharf in chains and photographs taken. In chains from 11 A. M. until 4 P. M. At Deer Island prisoners were kept in cells without any sanitary conveniences whatever for three days; corroborated other evidence of witness Mack as to conditions on Deer Island.

Oluf L. Root: Immigration Inspector; testified that prisoners brought from Fitchburg to Boston were handcuffed two and two together with a long chain between the two lines; chains and handcuffs remained on the prisoners while they were on the train and until he delivered them to the Deer Island boat. Raids in his district began at 5 minutes past one on the morning of January 3rd and were completed at 4 o'clock that morning; the persons arrested being taken out of their beds.

James A. Sullivan: Deputy Commissioner, testified that visitors were not allowed to see the aliens on Deer Island for one week after their arrival, nor was it easy for the aliens to send out any mail for the first three or four days after arrival. Witness protested that exposing the aliens to photographers while in chains had *not* been done by the Department of *Labor*.

Notes: (1) At the date of this report briefs have just been submitted in the Colyer case. Although Judge Anderson has not yet, therefore rendered a formal decision, he stated at the trial that unless the Government persuaded him to change his view he did not regard the Communist Party as one advocating force and violence.

(2) Secretary of Labor Wilson has held, since the Colyer case, that the Communist Labor Party does not advocate force and violence. He held the contrary, last January, as to the Communist Party. The Department of Justice raids were made, before either of these decisions, indiscriminately upon persons suspected of affiliation with either party.

EXHIBIT 14.

UNITED STATES SUPREME COURT.

SILVERTHORNE LUMBER COMPANY, INC., and FREDERICK W. SILVERTHORNE, Plaintiffs in Error,

vs.

UNITED STATES OF AMERICA.

Opinion by Mr. Justice Holmes—Decided January 26, 1920.

Mr. Justice Holmes delivered the opinion of the court:

*　　　*　　　*　　　*　　　*　　　*　　　*

The facts are simple. An indictment upon a single specific charge having been brought against the two Silverthornes mentioned, they both were arrested at their homes early in the morning of February 25, and were detained in custody a number of hours. While they were thus detained representatives of the Department of Justice and the United States marshal, without a shadow of authority, went to the office of their company and made a clean sweep of all the books, papers, and documents found there. All the employees were taken or directed to go to the office of the district attorney of the United States, to which also the books, etc., were taken at once. An application was made as soon as might be to the district court for a return of what thus had been taken unlawfully. It was opposed by the district attorney so far as he had found evidence against the plaintiffs in error, and it was stated that the evidence so obtained was before the grand jury. * * * Photographs and copies of material papers were made and a new indictment was framed, based upon the knowledge thus obtained. The district court ordered a return of the originals, but impounded the photographs and copies. * * *

The government now, while in form repudiating and condemning the illegal seizure, seeks to maintain its right to avail itself of the knowl-edge obtained by that means which otherwise it would not have had.

The proposition could not be presented more nakedly. It is that although of course its seizure was an outrage which the government now regrets, it may study the papers before it returns them, copy them, and then may use the knowledge that it has gained to call upon the owners in a more regular form to produce them; that the protection of the Constitution covers the physical possession, but not any advantages that the government can gain over the object of its pursuit by doing the forbidden act. * * * In our opinion such is not the law. It reduces the 4th Amendment to a form of words. 232 U. S. 393. The essence of a provision forbidding the acquisition of evidence in a certain way is that not merely evidence so acquired shall not be used before the court, but that it shall not be used at all. * * *

Judgment reversed.

The CHIEF JUSTICE and Mr. Justice Pitney dissent.

EXHIBIT 15.

U. S. DISTRICT COURT, DISTRICT OF MONTANA.

In the Matter of JOHN JACKSON.

Decision by JUDGE BOURQUIN, February 12, 1920.

BOURQUIN, J.: Petitioner, held for deportation as an alien "found advocating or teaching the unlawful destruction of property," and who at time of entry "was a person likely to become a public charge," seeks *habeas corpus* for that the evidence against him was unlawfully secured, that the deportation proceedings were unfair, and that the evidence fails to support the findings quoted above. Respondent returns the record of said proceedings.

Therefrom it appears that from August, 1918, to February, 1919, the Butte union of the Industrial Workers of the World was dissatisfied with working places, conditions and wages in the mining industry, and to remedy them were discussing ways and means, including a strike if necessary. In consequence its hall and orderly meetings were several times raided by employers' agents, federal agents and soldiers duly officered, acting by federal authority and without warrant. The members, men and women, many of whom a familiar principle concludes are citizens of the United States, made no resistance save oral protests, no retaliation, and there was no disorder save by the raiders. These, armed, forcibly entered, broke and destroyed property; searched effects and papers; seized papers and documents; cursed, insulted, beat, dispersed, and bayonneted members by order of the captain commanding; likewise entered petitioner's adjacent living apartments, insulted his wife, searched and seized his papers, several times arrested him and others, and in general in an orderly and populous city, perpetrated an orgy of terror, violence and crime against citizens and aliens in public assemblage, whose only offense seems to have been peaceable insistence upon an exercise of a clear legal right * * * These pamphlets and papers so seized from the hall and the petitioner's apartment, are the only material and vital evidence against him so far as the first finding quoted is concerned. * * *

Permitting all discussion of the contents of these pamphlets, and having in mind the political control over aliens, the summary character of the proceedings in deportation, and the limited jurisdiction of the courts in respect thereof, it is believed the deportation proceedings aforesaid were unfair in that they violated the searches and seizures and due process clauses of the Constitution, to the protection of which as a resident alien, petitioner is entitled. * * *

The Declaration of Independence, the writings of the Fathers of our Country, the Revolution, the Constitution and the Union, all were inspired to overthrow the like governmental tyranny. They are yet living, vital, potential forces to safeguard all domiciled in the country, aliens as well as citizens.

If evidence of the alien's evil advocacy and teaching is so wanting that it exists in only that herein, and as secured herein, he is a far less danger to this country than are the parties who in violation of law and order, of humanity and justice, have brought him to deportation. They are the spirit of intolerance incarnate, and the most alarming manifestation in America today.

Thoughtful men who love this country and its institutions see more danger in them and in their practices and the government by hysteria they stimulate, than in the miserable, hated "Reds" that are the ostensible occasion of them all. Those people may confidently assume that, even as the "Reds," they too in due time will pass, and the nation still live. It is for the courts to deal with both, to hold both in check when brought within the jurisdiction. * * *

The writ is granted.

EXHIBIT 16.

April 10, 1920.

DEPARTMENT OF LABOR

Office of the Secretary

WASHINGTON

DECISION OF LOUIS F. POST, ASSISTANT SECRETARY OF LABOR, in re Thomas Truss.

(Decision Given in Full. Italics by the Editor.)

This alien, a Pole by birth, is 33 years of age; he arrived in the United States in 1907, was married in 1912, and has three American-born children. He is a coat presser by occupation, earning about $40 a week and is or recently was president of the amalgamated clothing workers of Baltimore. His character, well attested by highly responsible witnesses, is that of a man who is not in the slightest degree dangerous to this government or at all inimical to any organized government, but who would make a good citizen of the United States. He was taken into custody on the 7th of January, 1920, by policemen who came to his home and asked him to accompany them for the purpose of answering questions. He complied, expecting to return presently. *The policemen conducted him to a police station where they delivered him to the police official in charge, saying that he was wanted by a special agent of the Bureau of Investigation of the U. S. Department of Justice. Thereupon the alien was locked in a cell over night, and until sometime during the next day his wife and friends were ignorant of his whereabouts. If there was any warrant for this arrest the alien was not shown the warrant or in any other way informed of the reason or the authority for his summary imprisonment, nor has any such authority been since disclosed. While still imprisoned he was examined on the 8th of January by a special agent of the Department of Justice and his examination reduced to writing. No lawful authority for this proceeding was disclosed to the alien at the time, nor has any been disclosed since; no warning was given him that his replies might be used against him, and he was not informed of his right to have counsel present to represent him if he wished.*

A special agent of the Bureau of Investigation of the Department of Justice thereupon made an affidavit in which he swore that in the course of his personal investigations and those of the officials and employees under his supervision and direction, he was informed and verily believed that the alien was a subject of Russia, that he was a member of the Communist Party and the Union of Russian Workers, but these organizations advocate the overthrow by force or violence of the Government of the United States, and that the alien was a member of and affiliated with them; that he was an anarchist, believed in and advocated the overthrow by force or violence of the Government, disbelieved in, and was opposed to all organized government. This affidavit was evidently a filled-out form, as the attorneys for the alien state; but inasmuch as the Secretary of Labor had already decided that the Union of Russian Workers and the Communist Party are within the proscription of the act of Congress of October 16, 1918, its averments imposed upon the Immigrant Inspector in Charge at Baltimore the duty of applying to the Secretary of Labor for a warrant of arrest (see Immigration Rule 22, Subdivision 3) and the Secretary of Labor was thereupon in duty bound to issue the warrant (see Section 19 of the Immigration Act of 1917, and Section 2 of the supplementary Act of October 16, 1918).

Accordingly, on January 8, the alien being then still in custody at the police station in Baltimore as stated above, the Immigrant Inspector in Charge at Baltimore telegraphed to his superior officer at Washington that satisfactory probable cause had been shown against the alien for membership in the Union of Russian Workers and the Communist Party. On the following day, January 9, a warrant of arrest was consequently issued by the Secretary of Labor and the Inspector in Charge at Baltimore was duly instructed by telegram to arrest the alien and hold him to bail in $1,000, the usual sum in such cases. In due course the formal warrant of arrest was transmitted to the Inspector in Charge at Baltimore, and on January 9, *two days after the arrest described above,* the alien was taken into the custody of the Department of Labor by the Inspector in Charge.

Prior thereto the Department of Labor was in no wise a participant in or directly or indirectly responsible for the arrest of the alien or his treatment in any respect. Subsequent, however, to January 9, and until he gave bail on January 15, the alien remained in custody as a prisoner upon the aforesaid warrant of the Department of Labor. His hearing pursuant thereto began January 20, and on April 1 the record of hearing came to the Assistant Secretary for decision pursuant to his authority under the Immigration laws and the organic act of the Department of Labor.

Examination of this record makes it evident that alien is not a Communist. Neither is he an anarchist. He is the opposite of an anarchist, namely, a socialist.

It also appears from the record that the alien came to the United States in 1907, has lived in Baltimore ever since, and has been for several years a respected member of and active worker for the St. Paul's Polish Church (Presbyterian) of Baltimore in which he is an elder.

As to his membership in the I. W. W., a point of contention at the alien's hearing, the record shows that he was a member of a branch of that organization six years ago, this branch being then the only union of wage workers in his shop; but that he joined the Amalgamated Clothing Workers when it was organized and thereupon dropped out of the I. W. W.

The record also shows that alien was for a time a member of a Russian Workers' organization, then an educational and mutual benefit society having nothing to do with governmental problems. This organization merged into the Union of Russian Workers (an organization heretofore proscribed under the act of October 16, 1918), whereupon the alien dropped his membership. He never became a member of the Union of Russian Workers.

The case appearing in the record against the alien turns, therefore, upon the question of his alleged membership in the Communist Party of America, which, like the Union of Russian Workers is under the ban of the act of October 16, 1918. He is shown to have authorized the signing by another for him of a printed application for membership in the Communist Party. Inasmuch, however, as that signing was prior to the organization of the proscribed Communist Party of America, it is a nullity for the purpose of this proceeding unless confirmed by activities or declarations of the alien after the constitution of the proscribed Communist Party was adopted and brought to his attention.

According to the circumstances shown alien's membership application was made in June, July or August, 1919. The Communist Party of America was not organized until September. Alien had authorized his ante-organization application at the suggestion of an official organizer of the Socialist Party at a mass meeting which alien attended upon the organizer's invitation, and at which the organizer set on foot preliminary proceedings for organizing a local branch of the subsequently organized Communist Party. As alien understood him the new party was to stand for socialization of mines, railroads, etc., thereby lowering prices as the Government Post Office had lowered postage.

Such a branch was informally organized, and on September 5, the day of the organization of the Communist Party in Chicago, it applied for a charter. The application was approved by Communist Party officials at Chicago on September 14 and a membership card was given to the alien. Having previously paid a membership fee and two months' dues the alien was credited with payments up to and including November. A charter was received by the secretary of the branch but not accepted by the group. The reason for delay seems to have been that no constitution nor any explanation of the purpose of the new party had been received, although the informally organized branch had been promised the attendance of an organizer to explain the Communist Party to its members. At a meeting in October, no organizer having come nor any constitution of the party, and the members of the branch not having learned anything more about the organization than had been explained at the mass meeting held in Baltimore before the Communist Party was organized, alien's branch decided to have no more meetings and instructed the secretary to return the charter. Its members never got together again.

On the basis of those circumstances, the responsibility falls upon this Department of deciding whether or not the alien comes within the membership clause of the Act of Congress of October 16, 1918.

Under that clause aliens must be deported if "they are members of or affiliated with" the Communist Party of America. If this clause be construed as meaning that aliens who have once technically become members of the Communist Party must be deported even though they had no guilty knowledge, or that the principle of "once a member always a member" applies, it might be possible to spell out from the circumstances described above a membership for which deportation would be mandatory. Even then, however, there would be no little difficulty without disregarding every principle of personal responsibility. Having applied for membership before the proscribed organization was born, and withdrawn before its constitution was brought even perfunctorily to his attention, this alien would seem to a fair American mind to lack the requisites even of technical membership. If, however, the requisites of technical membership were all present, nevertheless the Congress of the United States should not hastily be presumed to have intended that resident aliens be arrested and deported as members of an unlawful organization, when all the circumstances show the alien himself to have been innocent of any guilty knowledge or motive in taking membership and when it appears not only that he is and has been wholly free from any hostile purpose toward this Government, but that he is sympathetic with our democratic institutions.

Some members of Congress may possibly have intended, when they voted for this law, to have it construed in a narrow and un-American fashion; but it would not be reasonable to infer that Congress, as the Constitutional law-making body of this country, enacted this law with any such un-American purpose. I shall therefore assume in this case, as I have in a large number of similar cases, that Congress intended the Act of October 16, 1918, to be considered reasonably with reference to the individual knowledge and intent of persons drawn innocently into an unlawful membership.

If the act be so construed, this alien is not within the spirit of the act even if he were within its letter. In fact, however, he does not appear to be within its letter. Under the circumstances disclosed by the record he was never so much as a technical member of the proscribed Communist Party; and in so far as his conduct might be supposed to confirm his ante-organization application or to bring him within the affiliation clause of the act, the circumstances of his withdrawal are conclusive.

I have described this case at length because in most if not all essentials it is typical of a large proportion of fully 1,000 cases I have decided after hearings in which warrants of arrest had been issued by the Department of Labor on prima facie proof of probable cause furnished by special agents of the Bureau of Investigation of the Department of Justice. The aliens are arrested and imprisoned; while imprisoned they are subjected to a police-office inquisition; an affidavit showing probable cause (upon information and belief) is thereupon presented to the Department of Labor, whereupon the Department of Labor issues its warrant of arrest, takes over the custody of the alien, as by law it is required to do, and proceeds as usual in warrant cases under the expulsion clause of the immigration law. When the hearings at Immigration Stations are reported verbatim in regular course to the Department of Labor, the Secretary of Labor (or his lawful representative) who is charged with the exclusive responsibility, comes to examine these records, *it is found in a large proportion of the large number of cases I have examined that there is no better reason for deportation than is disclosed in the present case.* In some cases the membership is "automatic," the arrested alien having been transferred from a lawful organization to the unlawful one by vote of a group or branch of the former and without his knowledge. In some cases he has had knowledge of the transfer but none at all of the character of the organization to which he has been transferred. In other cases he has signed applications before the existence of the unlawful organization and has never confirmed his membership by any conscious act. Sometimes an organizer or a friend has signed the application for him. *As a rule, the hearings show the aliens arrested to be working men of good character who have never been arrested before, who are not anarchists or revolutionists, nor politically or otherwise dangerous in any sense. Many of them, as in this case, have American-born children. It is pitiful to consider the hardships to which they and their families have been subjected during the past three or four months by arbitrary arrest, long detention in default of bail beyond the means of hard working wage earners to give, for nothing more dangerous than affiliating with friends of their own race, country and language, and without the slightest indication of sinister motive, or any unlawful act within their knowledge or intention.* To permit aliens to violate the hospitality of this country by conspiring against it is something which no American can contemplate with patience. *Equally impatient, however, must any patriotic American be with drastic proceedings on flimsy proof to deport aliens who are not conspiring against our laws and do not intend to.* Although these are not criminal proceedings, being wholly administrative in their character, their effect upon the innocent individual who in this summary way is found to be guilty is as distressing to him and his family, to his friends and to his neighbors, as the effect of conviction for crime by regular judicial processes.

It is sometimes difficult to draw the line in the records of cases of aliens charged with membership in a proscribed organization—and very few cases so far instituted upon probable cause shown by special agents of the Bureau of Investigation are for anything else—between those who are members understandingly and those whose membership is only technical and without guilty knowledge on their part. The natural association of alien residents with their own countrymen and the overlapping of social, industrial and political organizations, each with its factions, tend to confuse the circumstances. As a guide through this maze, I have tried to follow the following principles of decision in each individual case:

1. The Communist Party of America is within the membership clauses of the Act of October 16, 1918. (Secretary's memorandum in the Preis case.)

2. Personal signing of the application for membership required by the Communist Party as quoted in the Secretary's memorandum in the Preis case, when such signing is supplemented by circumstances indicating membership subsequent to the creation of the Communist Party, constitutes membership within the purview of the Act of October 16, 1918.

3. Signing by another with the authority of the alleged member has the same effect as personal signing, provided authority to sign and understanding of the purpose thereof are proved.

4. Applications for membership not confirmed by acceptance do not constitute membership within the Act of October 16, 1918, unless it may be inferred from further facts indicative thereof.

5. Name in a membership list is not in itself proof of membership.

6. "Automatic membership" does not constitute membership within the Act of October 16, 1918, unless supported by proof of individual activities or declarations tending to show knowledge of the character of the organization.

7. Signed applications antedating the formation of the Communist Party (on or about September 5, 1919), which are not unlawful in their own terms or their legitimate implications, do not in themselves constitute proof of membership nor of application for membership in the proscribed Communist Party.

8. When membership has been withdrawn under circumstances satisfactorily establishing good faith, the accused alien does not come within the proscriptions of the Act of October 16, 1918, as to membership.

9. When the accused alien appears to be a person of good general character, fit for American citizenship except for the accusation in hand, and there is reasonable doubt of his membership, the warrant of arrest will be cancelled.

10. Statements of the accused alien, whether oral or in writing made while he is in custody and without opportunity fairly afforded him from the beginning to be represented by counsel, and without clear warning that anything he says may be used against him will be disregarded pursuant to the principle Re Jackson (U. S. District Court for Montana, Bourquin, J.) and of Silverthorne vs. U. S. (January 28, 1920), as having been unlawfully obtained.

11. Exhibits seized upon the premises or the person of the accused alien without lawful process, will be disregarded pursuant both to the principle and the precise decision in Re Jackson and Silverthorne vs. U. S.

12. In cases in which the alien is the father of children born in the United States, and therefore constitutional American citizens, and who are dependent upon and receive from him parental support, every fair doubt regarding membership within the purview of the statute will be accorded.

Guided by those principles, I am of opinion that upon the record in this case the alien is not a member of or affiliated with the Communist Party or any other proscribed organization within the meaning of the Act of Congress of October 16, 1918.

The warrant is cancelled.

LOUIS F. POST,
Assistant Secretary.

Note by the Editor: The rendering of the foregoing decision was the principal reason for the effort in the House of Representatives to institute impeachment proceedings against Mr. Post.

EXHIBIT 17.

PROPAGANDA LETTER, ATTORNEY GENERAL TO MAGAZINES.

Office of the Attorney General.

Washington, D. C., January 27, 1920.

—— and Associates, Editor —— Magazine, New York City.

DEAR —— :

In order that as one of the leaders of thought of this country you may have before you an authentic source of information as to the significance of the present situation I am taking the liberty of sending to you photostatic copies of original documents published by various branches of the Communist Press in Russia and in the United States. These furnish the purpose, history, and character of the Red Radical Movement, not by hearsay, but under the authoritative sanction of its own progenitors.

Exhibit No. 1 is the Report of Louis C. Fraina, International Secretary of the Communist Party of America, describing fully its antecedents, birth and projects, and follows the form of an application of the Communist Party of America to be accepted in the Bureau of the Communist International as a "major party."

Exhibit No. 2 is the manifesto of the Third Communist International adopted at Moscow, March 2-6, 1919, and signed by Comrades C. Rakovsky, N. Lenin, M. Zinerzen, L. Trotsky and Fritz Platten. It is an exhaustive statement of the rationale, principles and program of Russian Bolshevism and its ambition for world-wide dominion.

Exhibit No. 3 is the responsive and cooperating Manifesto, Constitution and Program of the Communist Party of America.

Exhibit No. 4 represents the form of application for membership in this party, containing the pledge to active enlistment in its seditious work.

Exhibit No. 5 gives the Novomirski Manifesto of the Anarchist-Communists organized in the Federation of Unions of Russian Workers of the United States and Canada, similar in purpose to the manifestoes of previously numbered exhibits and containing particularly the declaration "We are atheists; we are communists; we are anarchists."—You all have one task—to destroy the world of gain and create a world of freedom; for all there is one means—an armed insurrection and forcible seizure of all instruments and all products of toil. "Woe to the enemies of the laboring class."

[NOTE.—This paragraph is deliberately false in its implication; although the document was reprinted in New York it was written in Odessa in 1905 for the purposes of the Russian Revolution of that year.]

Exhibit No. 6. "Your Shop" is an evidence of the sabotizing of labor and labor enemies prescribed on the communist program.

Exhibit No. 7. The State-Strike Breaker, of like use but aimed at the defamation of government and the employing class.

Exhibit No. 8. A proclamation of the Communist International against the Versailles Peace, designed to exert influence toward its failure of ratification.

Exhibit No. 9. An example of the Russian Bolshevik propaganda among our soldiers in Siberia.

Striking passages in these exhibits are marked for convenience.

The whole is submitted for the furtherance of a more realizing popular appreciation of the menace involved in the unrestrained spread of criminal Communism's unspeakable social treason among the masses.

It is the contention of the Department of Justice that these documents standing alone demonstrate:

(1) That the present aim of the Russian Government and its officers is to foment and incite discontent, aiming toward a revolution in this country.

[NOTE.—The Department has not yet been able to prove this charge in the Martens deportation proceedings.]

(2) That the entire movement is a dishonest and criminal one, in other words, an organized campaign to acquire the wealth and power of all countries for the few agitators and their criminal associates.

[NOTE.—The entire movement is one of orthodox extreme Socialism along the lines of the Karl Marx Manifesto of 1848.]

The Red Movement does not mean an attitude of protest against alleged defects in our present political and economic organization of society. It does not represent the radicalism of progress. It is not a movement of liberty-loving persons. Lenine himself made the statement, at the Third Soviet Conference, "Among one hundred so-called Bolsheviks there is one real Bolshevik, thirty-nine criminals, and sixty fools." It advocates the destruction of all ownership in property, the destruction of all religion and belief in God. It is a movement organized against Democracy, and in favor of the power of the few built by force. Bolshevism, syndicalism, the Soviet Government, sabotage, etc., are only names for old theories of violence and criminality.

Having lived at the expense of the Russian people for two years, these speculators in human lives and other peoples' earnings are trying to move to new fields to the East and to the West, hoping to take advantage of the economic distress and confusion of mind in which humanity finds itself after the terrific strain of five years of war.

Its sympathizers in this country are composed chiefly of criminals, mistaken idealists, social bigots, and many unfortunate men and women suffering with various forms of hyperesthesia.

This Department, as far as existing laws allows, intends to keep up an unflinching war against this movement no matter how cloaked or dissembled. We are determined that this movement will not be permitted to go far enough in this country to disturb our peace or create any widespread distrust of the people's government.

Our actions have been and will be continuously met with criticism. In so far as that it is founded upon an understanding of these documents and upon the situation which they disclose, we welcome it, but the sabotizing of public thought is an essential of this movement, and we are asking you, after reading these documents, to aid in seeing that the American people are not misled. The natural sympathy of our people for distress in all forms is now being used by the friends of Bolshevism in discussing the number of women and children alleged to have been left dependent by our deportations. We can assure you that the condition of the family of each and every person arrested has been personally examined into by the Agents of this Department, and that wherever there are dependents of these men they are being individually looked after by the most prominent charitable organizations of their own creed in their locality.

[NOTE.—This statement of fact is of course substantially false.]

It is no part of the Attorney General's duty to look after the families of violators of our laws. Hundreds of thousands of men are in prisons throughout our country without it ever having been urged by anyone that the Government is under any proper charge to look after the families brought into distress through criminal acts of their own members.

But in order that the issue may remain clear, we have determined to see to it that no woman or child be allowed to suffer for the conduct of their supporters.

Their next move has been to agitate criticism of the Government's activity as directed against the right of free speech. I yield to no one in my anxiety that that right be preserved unclouded and unquestioned, but nothing so endangers the exercise of a right as the abuse thereof, and a clear definition of the right of free speech and of a free press sufficiently answers any criticism of the necessity which the Government finds itself under in combating this movement. I ask you to consider the following definition of this right, taken from our courts and from the great leaders in the battle of the centuries for that right.

[The Attorney General then discusses various legal authorities on the subject of free speech.]

The Department of Justice has a vast amount of other information regarding the radical movement in this country, which is at your disposal. It will give me much pleasure to have one of your representatives call at this office so that you may obtain the information first-hand. If you are unable to send a representative, I will be glad to furnish you with any details, either general or in specific cases.

[NOTE.—If a private lawyer were to try his "specific cases" in the press in this manner he would be in danger of disbarment.]

My one desire is to acquaint people like you with the real menace of evil-thinking which is the foundation of the Red movement.

Respectfully,
(Signed)   A. MITCHELL PALMER.

EXHIBIT 18.

PROPAGANDA PAGE OF DEPARTMENT OF JUSTICE.

In late January or February, 1920, there was sent out to country newspapers a specimen newspaper service page of news stories and cartoons carrying at the top the following caption:

"Plates of material shown below are furnished to you without charge, carriage prepaid, on the order of U. S. Department of Justice, Washington, D. C. The metal remains our property to be returned in the usual manner.

(Sgd.)   WESTERN NEWSPAPER UNION."

In the center of the page is a cartoon reproduced from the New York Tribune and entitled "Give the American Blue Grass a Show." This represents Uncle Sam as a farmer weeding up thistles, each of which has a theatrical Bolshevik head, and loading them into a basket labeled "Deportation of the Reds," while in the background a woman labeled "America" is sowing grass seed.

The principal column at the left hand side has the following copy-heads: "WARNS NATION OF RED PERIL—U. S. Department of Justice Urges Americans to Guard Against Bolshevism Menace—CALLS RED PLANS CRIMINAL—Press, Church, Schools, Labor Unions and Civic Bodies Called Upon to Teach True Purpose of Bolshevist Propaganda." The story under this begins:

"Washington.—Calling for the patriotic support of all true Americans in its fight to protect their homes, religion and property from the spreading menace of Bolshevism, the U. S. Department of Justice has issued a warning against the insidious propaganda of the 'Reds' during the New Year. It reads:"——

Then follows a statement generally similar to parts of the Attorney General's letter, Exhibit 17.

A double width column in the center of the page under the cartoon carries the following copy head: "TO 'CONQUER AND DESTROY STATE,' U. S. COMMUNISTS CALL FOR LABOR REVOLT—Revolutionary Pamphlet, Found in U. S. Department of Justice Investigation, Gives Message of Communists in Chicago to Russian Headquarters." There follow extracts from the Manifesto and Program, etc., of the Communist Party, of the character which judges and juries, in States having criminal anarchy or criminal syndicalism laws, have sent men to jail for five to ten years for printing. It is not perceived how the country newspapers could have reprinted this material without becoming amenable to criminal prosecution, and it is an interesting legal question whether the action of the Attorney General in supplying the material was not instigation to the commission of a crime.

The right hand column is also double width and carries the following caption: "'OVERTHROW WORLD ORDER!' CRY COMMUNISTS—Manifesto of Communist International, Seized in U. S. Department of Justice Raids, Tells 'Reds' Own Story of Their Plans for World Wide Plunder." There follow under this extracts from the Manifesto of the Communist Internationale. The remarks in the last paragraph as to the legality of such publication apply here also.

Below is reprinted a piece of I. W. W. verse entitled "WHAT REDS WOULD HAVE US SING—From I. W. W. Songs—Seized in Red Raids of U. S. Department of Justice." There is nothing whatever illegal about the verses quoted except that they violate the laws of versification.

At the foot of the right hand column under the caption "MEN LIKE THESE WOULD RULE YOU," are pictures of four alleged Communist agitators "Deported by U. S. Department of Justice" (Deported as matter of fact and law by the U. S. Department of Labor) which alleged agitators look very much as any member of society might look if he had been jailed and not been allowed to wash or shave for some days.

A facsimile of this page offered free to country newspapers at the expense of the Department of Justice may be seen in The Nation, New York, issue of March 6, 1920.

EXHIBIT 19.

"Lest We Forget"

FIRST TO CAPTURE A HUN

Blazikowisky and Cochansky, Yankees from Michigan, Won the Honor.

Washington, Feb. 12.—The first German prisoner taken by American forces was captured by Adam Blazikowiski and John Cochanski of Ironwood, Mich., Representative James of Michigan, was informed today by Adjutant General Harris. * * *

(*Boston Transcript, Feb. 12, 1920.*)